PAIN AND ADVERSITY
SAVED MY LIFE

HOW TO TURN PAIN INTO TRIUMPH—ADVERSITY INTO OPPORTUNITY

"I LOST SOMEONE FOR A WHILE; THAT SOMEONE WAS ME."

JOURNEY BEYOND THE ORDINARY—MY RICH LIFE EXPERIENCES

PDF INSPIRES

I am not great because I follow a script;
I am great because I am the script.
—Paul D. Forgay

ISBN 978-1-63630-585-1 (Paperback)
ISBN 978-1-63630-417-5 (Hardcover)
ISBN 978-1-63630-418-2 (Digital)

Covenant Books, Inc.
11661 Hwy 707
Murrells Inlet, SC 29576
www.covenantbooks.com

To my sister Robin: an amazing sister, mom, daughter, aunt, and friend—you will forever have a place in my heart! May you rest in peace!

Love, your proud brother, Paul

Contents

CHAPTER 1

INSPIRATIONAL LIFE EXPERIENCES

> *I am not great because I follow a script; I*
> *am great because I am the script.*
> —*Paul D. Forgay*

> *When writing the story of your life,*
> *don't let anyone else hold the pen.*
> —*Harley Davidson*

What if something suddenly happened to me? What mark would I leave on this earth once I am tossed into the abyss? It's an interesting question of which I have no concrete answer for. Writing is my passion; it's what I love doing every day. So maybe, just maybe, the swift stroke of a pen is the mark I've been searching for.

JOURNEY BEYOND THE ORDINARY—
MY RICH LIFE EXPERIENCES

Sometimes we read books about how to be like someone else. This book doesn't mirror that, it is about having the prowess to be you and not what others want you to be. It has always been a dream of mine to write a book—and not just any book, but a book that would impact others' lives in a hopeful, inspirational, purposeful way. I envisioned a book of substance and meaning that would truly matter to people, filled with my own inspirational life experiences. I wanted to write a book on my own so that I may convey my heartfelt emotions and immense passion. I refused to have someone else (a.k.a. a ghostwriter) write about my Journey Beyond the Ordinary—My Rich Life Experiences.

What is a ghostwriter? They are paid to do research and write for someone else. Ghostwriters write memoirs, fiction, and nonfiction books. Varying on the assignment, they will write making use of their client's name or be recognized as a collaborator. The clients of ghostwriters are typically extremely active people—entrepreneurs, business executives, celebrities, athletes—who want to write a book but do not have the time or aptitude to do so. So they hire someone else to do it for them. I believed that I would be doing myself and my readers a disfavor by allowing a ghostwriter to write for me, after all I hold the pen for my own script. If I allowed a ghostwriter to write my book, yes, the book would have more content, look extremely charming; but like in most cases, it would be filled with a variety of meaningless rhetoric. I choose to hold the pen and write the story of my life because I am my own script. I knew that I had to be courageous enough to share the trials and tribulations I've had to overcome in order to make my dreams become a reality.

> *Never stop pursuing your dreams; sometimes*
> *they're the only things that keep us sane.*
> *—Paul D. Forgay*

Growing up, I was not like everyone else; I was unique and often felt lonely in a crowded room. I was self-conscious about being labeled stupid, an also-ran, crazy, a loser, or a failure. As I grew up, I wanted to better understand what pushed me, gave me energy and willpower. It became important to me to take a step back and assess my life, including those I may have inadvertently hurt along the way. I thought about this a lot, and it bothered me. I discovered that I was far from perfect and that I had inadvertently created adverse situations for others in both my business life and personal life. I wanted to dig deep within myself to see just how I let myself, family and friends down. I mention this because it's important to understand that your own hardships can take a toll not only on yourself but also on those around you.

> *Why have I always done what I do with so much*
> *passion, a tenacious work ethic and humility?*
> *Because I had to prove to myself that I am not*
> *stupid, an also-ran, crazy, a loser, or a failure.*
> —*Paul D. Forgay*

I believe everyone has their own personal, profound *why*: Why do you do what you do? Why do you do it passionately, with a distinct purpose? I am exceptionally passionate about my *why*—to the point that it still has the power to bring tears to my eyes. Why do I do what I do with so much passion, a tenacious work ethic, and humility? To prove to myself that I am not all the things I was labeled with growing up. My *why* also includes the three most amazing God-given gifts one can ever wish for: my son, Luke, and my daughters Naomi and Hannah. I emphatically believe that If your *why* doesn't bring you to tears, it's just a mere thought and not your personal and passionate *why*.

Hannah (daughter), Luke (son), Naomi (daughter)

I need my family and friends to know the real me, my story, and that it is okay to be different. I want my personal life experiences to move others so profoundly that they too can stop feeling lonely in a crowded room.

Adversity is not the enemy or a dream killer. It is
a character builder and personal growth advisor.
—*Paul D. Forgay*

***

I decided early in life that I could defy any obstacle in my path. I knew I could achieve greatness and be of service to others because I was unique, special, and believed in myself. I knew I possessed exceptional skills, a relentless work ethic, talent, heart, faith, and courage. I was convinced that I had no limitations and that I was my own greatest asset. I want to tell you a little more about my life to illustrate how that came to be.

The lyrics to "Different" Micah Taylor has inspired me—it boasts a positive and deeply meaningful message

I grew up in a two-bedroom, one-bath rental in a rough and diverse neighborhood in North Long Beach, California. I shared a room no bigger than ten feet by ten feet with my brother, sister, and three cousins (lived with us from time to time). My mother was pregnant with me at seventeen. Both of my parents (and their parents) were high school dropouts, and we would do anything we had to do to make ends meet. I remember driving down alley ways sitting in the back of our yellow Ford Torino with the window down. We would stop and go through trash cans looking for clothes, pans, tools—anything we could use.

Paul's Childhood Neighborhood

Success is not a theory, science or secret.
The pathway to success is hard work,
determination, perseverance, and something
most commonly known as sweat equity.
—*Paul D. Forgay*

I had a choice to make: do I allow my unfortunate circumstances dictate who I am as a person, allow them to crush my spirit and my dreams beyond the point of no return. Or do I use these circumstances as an investment for my future? It's been my experience that investing in personal growth, albeit through failure in some cases are an investment that if utilized properly is something money can never buy!

Paul's Childhood Neighborhood

It takes courage to address things in our lives that we are ashamed of or don't have the fortitude to talk about. Being brave is something that can't be taught in a classroom or read from a book. It's something that inspires you to do the right thing at the right time without thinking about it. Fearlessness and bravery often go hand in hand because they involve taking action when it is difficult—even scary—to do so. Being courageous might involve, leaving home at the age of seventeen with nothing but your clothes and never looking back, or taking on a task so daunting that it makes you cringe just thinking about it.

Paul

The first thing is, to be honest with yourself.
You can never have an impact on the
world if you have not changed yourself.
—Nelson Mandela

I have experienced failure and adversity on a multitude of levels during the course of my life. I have lived in my car, dug through trash cans, and faced physical and mental abuse. I have dealt with bipolar disorder and attention-deficit hyperactivity disorder, family violence, failed relationships, and substance abuse. I have contemplated suicide. I have made millions and lost millions. My story is one of humility, persistence, determination, passion, grit, gratitude, and faith. I have endured and prevailed over my hardships with courage, a relentless work ethic, faith and prayer that I could realize my true potential.

Lazy people excel in the ability to blame
others for their lack of success.
—Paul D. Forgay

Through all of my pain and suffering, I began to realize that I was better than I'd thought I was. That in itself gave me the confidence and courage to deal with and withstand my adversities. What you need to know is that I'm speaking from personal experience—not based on something I read in a book or learned in a classroom. The hardships I've endured throughout my life have given me the strength to How to Turn Pain into Triumph—Adversity into Opportunity. Adversity not only changed my life; it literally *saved* my life—and that's as real as it gets.

I was diagnosed with bipolar disorder, also known as manic-depressive illness. This is a brain disorder that can cause unusual shifts in mood, sleep too little, variation of activity levels, shortage of energy, and the ability to carry out day-to-day tasks. My specific diagnosis consists of both manic and depressive symptoms. This disorder can incapacitate one's ability to work or even do something as simple as getting out of bed in the morning; just about anything you can think of can be a struggle. I have experienced many sleepless nights thinking about gathering up the courage to break free from the merciless feeling of being lonely in a crowded room and the mental disorder I have that is exceptionally excruciating and most people who agonize from one would never wish it on anyone, lest of all themselves. The pain by no means surrenders, even in the stillness of the night.

You're not alone in the fight to control your mind.
—Paul D. Forgay

I also suffer from attention-deficit hyperactivity disorder, which complicated things even further. I rarely sleep, but when I do it is just for three or four hours a night. Mental illness never goes away, and if it's not managed, it can haunt you every second of every day for the rest of your life. I used to be ashamed to talk about my illnesses because I feared I would be labeled *maniacal, crazy*, and *abnormal.* The fact is, I am unique, special, and different, yet I am still standing.

I began to research, study, and learn about bipolar disorder and ADHD. I discovered that many leaders, many successful and famous people, have also been diagnosed or believed to be bipolar. These include Winston Churchill, Vincent Van Gogh, Ted Turner, Steve Jobs, Demi Lovato, Jim Carrey, Lady Gaga and Ernest Hemingway, to name just a few. That's not a bad group of individuals to share something so extraordinary with—even something like a mental illness. I chose to turn pain into triumph and adversity into opportunities that I'd never thought possible.

Skills, habits, and *attitude* have each played significant roles in my life and have helped me with struggles I never thought I would have to deal with. I have been able to use these tools to surpass my competition and confront personal and professional challenges. Understanding that *I am my greatest asset* has given me the confidence and courage to face adversity head-on, turn adverse situations into opportunities, and live a purposeful life.

As soon as life would get too much for me to handle, I dropped to my knees and pray. I wouldn't pray for the things I needed; I would pray for the things I am most thankful for: family, friends, humility, faith, failure, compassion, adversity, mercy, knowledge, grace, gratitude, pain, and love. I didn't always stick with God, but He always stuck with me!

It's been my experience that you can turn adversity into any kind of opportunity if you start by taking an inventory of your own unique *skills, habits*, and *attitude.* Once you've identified these, you can use them to your advantage, and you'll see and understand that *you are your greatest asset.* Challenge yourself; just go for it. Pray, believe in yourself, and don't just *exist*—because that's not *living!*

Naomi (daughter) , Hannah (daughter), Paul, Luke (son)

***

*No One Knows My Struggle They
Only See The Trouble.*
—*Tupac Shakur*

So…how am I still here to tell my story? That is the subject of this little book. My hope is that it inspires you to rise above whatever adversity you find yourself facing and live your best life. The first step is knowing deep down that if I could do it, you can too.

The important thing to understand is that mine is not just a story of hardship and challenge—it is a story of tenacity, work ethic, humility, persistence, determination, passion, grit, gratitude, and faith. These are the qualities that helped me discover my potential, endure, and prevail with courage and confidence. I am able to Turn Pain into Triumph and Adversity into Opportunity because I have built up a mental armor that will not allow anyone or anything to detour me from my dreams!

Thanks to my discovery of those qualities within myself, I graduated high school, enlisted in the military, graduated from an esteemed university, and built several thriving businesses.

More important than any of those things—or any material possessions that can be acquired in this world—God has blessed me with three amazing kids: Luke, Naomi, and Hannah. They inspire me every day, and I believe they are the reason I picked myself up and turned my destitution into a magnificent, joyous, and blessed life. The power of the human spirit is simply euphoric!

Paul (far left)—Army Basic Training

DEPARTMENT OF THE ARMY

CERTIFICATE OF TRAINING

This is to certify that

PRIVATE PAUL D. FORGAY

has successfully completed

Basic Training Cycle 48-82 on 5 November 1982

Company A, 4th Battalion
3d Basic Training Brigade
Given at Fort Dix, New Jersey 08640

WILLIAM F. KERLIN
CPT, ADA
Commanding

Paul—Army Certificate of Training

*Phenomenally successful people are
continually in search of greatness.*
                                    —Paul D. Forgay

In search of greatness, gratitude is king.
                                    —Paul D. Forgay

*Experience is not what happens to you; it's
what you do with what happens to you.*
                                    —Aldous Huxley

Definition of excuse; failure.
                                    —Paul D. Forgay

CHAPTER 2

FAMILY AND FRIENDS

Adversity is a miracle in disguise.
—Paul D. Forgay

I have often felt lonely in a crowded room. There
have been many times when I have wanted to tear
my chest open so that I could breathe. But through
it all, I have held my head high and sought the
strength that can only come from a tenacious work
ethic, faith, humility, gratitude, and prayer.
—Paul D. Forgay

On occasion, life can be chaotic, downright crazy, and at times feel like your world is deteriorating right in front of your eyes. It's during these challenging times that your genuine, innermost trusted family and friends rise to the occasion. I'm sure you've heard it been said before that you'll have many acquaintances throughout your lifetime but only a handful of remarkable family and friends that will forever have your back in the worst of times and the best of times. There's a song by Gavin DeGraw that really sums it up what it means to be a trusted family or friend: It's amazing how many friends you have when you have a lot of money.

The lyrics to "Soldier" Gavin DeGraw offer inspiration to me.

"Where did all the people go, they got scared. It's called the moment of truth. When times get harder people hiding everywhere. You get worried I'll be your soldier; you get hurt and I'll take your pain!"

When words fail music speaks.
—William Shakespeare

TURN PAIN INTO TRIUMPH AND ADVERSITY INTO OPPORTUNITY

I can tell you from experience that if it wasn't for the love, kindness, compassion, understanding, support from such incredible family members—Luke (son), Naomi (daughter), Hannah (daughter), Tahme R., Michelle V., Louis H., Nancy P., Robin W.(sister), trusted friends; Robin and Sandra J., Joe H., Scott E., David P., Laura T., Henry D., Ruben S., Oscar G., Mr. Shrotman "Coach," and Mrs. Shrotman—I would have never had the fortitude to rise above my circumstances. I firmly believe that without them, combined with my personal eight pillars of strength—courage, faith, gratitude, heart, humility, hustle, prayer, and relentless work ethic—I would have slipped away into a bottomless pit of nothingness. *"I lost someone for a while; that someone was me." Because of my remarkable family and friends, I'm extremely blessed that it was only for a while.*

Giving up is not in my DNA.
—Paul D. Forgay

Successful salespeople that possess expedient
problem solving skills accompanied by
a tenacious work ethic can turn pennies
into dollars in the blink of an eye.
—Paul D. Forgay

Growing up I would dream of becoming a father someday. People would ask me what I wanted to be when I grew up. My answer was always the same: a father. Not just any father, but everything my biological father was not. I made a point of being actively involved in my kids' lives and I was fortunate enough to do just that. One of the many rewards of being a parent is seeing and encouraging your children to go after their dreams and aspirations with a massive commitment to mastery, creativity, imagination, and a tenacious work ethic. The difference between reality and a dream is hard work and a never-giving-up attitude; this is exactly what I have instilled in my kids. I strongly encourage them to just go for it. There's nothing worse than going to a job every day that you despise. If you have the right attitude, you can achieve whatever it is that you want out of life. My response is always the same: how will you ever know unless you try? If money is one of your main objectives, it's important to identify your gift spend as much time as it takes to refine your craft; take it head on and the money will follow. I've tried to teach them that everything adverse can be used to benefit you, but you must be willing to develop even under tough, adverse circumstances, because this is where the growth happens. It's your life. Hold the pen and write your own script!

> *Fundamental conviction is my*
> *why is greater than me.*
> *—Paul D. Forgay*

I remember the day my son, Luke, was born; it was without a doubt one of the best days of my life. Luke is an amazing and handsome, smart, and athletic young man who has many talents: surf photographer, raced motorcycles, played football, just to name a few. Luke's passion is music. He is currently attending music school: Icon Collective in Burbank, California. He graduates from Icon Collective in December 2020 and I couldn't be more happy or proud of him.

Paul, Luke (son)

The day my daughter Naomi was born was most certainly one of the greatest days of my life. Her family and close friends call her Nay. She is an incredible young lady; she is beautiful, smart, loving, athletic, and one of the most caring people I have ever met in my life. She was cheerleader, played soccer and softball as a kid. Naomi is currently attending college, working as an EMT, and training to become a firefighter. I am immensely proud of her.

Paul, Naomi (daughter)

I will never forget the day my daughter Hannah was born. Since that day I've referred to her as "my little one" or my brown-eyed girl. She was a cheerleader and played softball as a kid. Hannah is currently attending the University of Alabama, studying for a career in the medical field. Hannah is a beautiful, intelligent, athletic, kind, and loving young lady with a bright future in front of her. I am extremely proud of her.

Paul, Hannah (daughter)

I couldn't be prouder of each of them, their achievements, and the young hard working, caring grown-ups they have become. I am honored and delighted to be their father.

Dreams really do come true!

> Happy birthday, dad. I love you so much. This past year or 2 I have learned a lot and I just want to say that I look up to you and admire you because you are such a great dad and provide so much for us and I wouldn't be able to live if something were to ever happen to you. You mean so much to me and I am so extremely thankful to have you as my dad. I am so blessed to be able to go to the school I do because I have gotten closer to Christ and the gospel and it has made me realize a lot in life and some stuff I learn at school really helps me get through things. I wouldn't be at this school if it wasn't for you. I can't thank you enough for getting me to olu. I wouldn't want to go anywhere else. The closer I have gotten to

Christ the more thankful and blessed I realized I am to have the life I do. I want to provide for my kids like you provide for us. You are my role model I love you so much. Don't stop what you're doing because you're a great dad and I hope you know that. Happy Birthday!! Thank you for everything. Hannah

Accepting mediocrity is a slow
and agonizing death.
—*Paul D. Forgay*

I found this at my sister Robin's house a few days before she passed away in September 2019:

It = my life experiences

Awhile, back I decided to write a book for a couple of reasons. But mainly because if I don't, it will just continue to roll around in my head (wash, rinse, repeat) and to share the humor I have found in the darkness. Because every time I think my life experiences interactions are "normal," I notice the look on people's faces staring back at me in pure shock (sheer terror).

We all have our own coping mechanisms in life—mine is to take the darkest, most unexpected moment and find humor in it, sometimes making others uncomfortable; but no matter how uncomfortable it makes them, I have realized that my being vulnerable helps most of them to feel more human!

I will always remember and cherish the numerous times we would sing "Rockin Robin" The Jackson Five

Thank you for the endearing memories

You have given me the strength and fearlessness to keep my dreams alive. Thank you for always believing in me!

Paul, Robin (sister)

I love you and miss you dearly, Your Proud Brother, Paul

There are things in my life that I am not very proud of. At times, I may have carelessly created challenging situations for both my trusted family members and my friends. It's important for me to recognize that my own hardships quite possibly took a toll on those I trusted the most; and for that, I am extremely apologetic for.

They're the main reason that I have the courage to write about the things I am most embarrassed about and at the same time most proud of. These amazing people didn't have to stick around, especially during times that they really didn't have to. These people are soldiers!

> *Without a strong work ethic and the deep-*
> *seated desire to succeed, you will lack the*
> *insight in realizing your full potential.*
> *—Paul D. Forgay*

> *It's your mind; don't grant anyone*
> *the luxury of contaminating it.*
> *—Paul D. Forgay*

TURN PAIN INTO TRIUMPH ~ ADVERSITY INTO OPPORTUNITY!

Chapter 3

Shatter Your Fears

*Shattering my fears, I was able to experience a
pure and inspiring epic journey of transformation.*
—*Paul D. Forgay*

*Hail to the man who went through life always
helping others, knowing no fear, and to whom
aggressiveness and resentment are alien. Such is the
stuff of which the great moral leaders are made.*
—*Albert Einstein*

Every day allows you a second chance to conquer your fears and make what you thought impossible, possible. I knew I would never achieve my purpose in life unless I obliterated **FEAR; F**alse **E**vidence **A**ppearing **R**eal. One of my greatest fears I had was exposing my brokenness, but I decided to expose myself as if the entire world was watching, knowing that someday I would break through my brokenness to reveal the strength and goodness I have within. I've also learned that fear can be a liar, so I promised myself that I was not going to fear the unfamiliar and that I refused to accept mediocrity because in my experience, mediocrity is just another word for average.

*Transformation through personal
life experiences is imminent.*
—*Paul D. Forgay*

I genuinely believe that we all have the capability to harness our own power: the power of our "greatest asset." Traveling the road to understanding and tapping into this power takes drive, self-efface-ment, creativity, consistency, and faith. Along that road, you may encounter a multitude of obstacles—as I did—and experience some dark and lonely days and nights—as I did. But I'll say it again: if I could emerge from the darkness as a whole, successful, blessed, hum-bled, grateful and fortunate person, you can do it too.

I have learned that in times of struggle and injustice, it is essential to be courageous and resilient in the presence of fear. I have learned over time that kindness, peace, and love have always persevered over hate and fear. Diversity is not only a system of measurement; it is an ingredient for success. Demand change. It has been my experience that there is enormous strength walking in solidarity, hand in hand, creating sweeping change and not just noise, but lasting equality!

I believe that everyone has a moral responsibility to do the right thing, even in the presence of fear!

PDF Banner

*Have the courage to stand up against
the atrocious injustice of racism.*
—Paul D. Forgay

Over the past several decades, I have written hundreds of brief affirmations that I hope can inspire and enlighten others. These thought-provoking words and my journey offer far more substance than the basic appreciation of cars, girls, and yachts that permeates the "sales inspo" industry.

You'll see these words of wisdom scattered throughout this book. I urge you to use them as a stepping stone and then come up with your own affirmations—words and ideas that are meaningful to you personally. Go back often to the thoughts that give you strength. Start each day by repeating a phrase or a few sentences that light your inner fire. Perhaps you'd like to start with this:

> *Walk fearlessly and crush the obscure*
> *shadows of mediocrity.*
> *—Paul D. Forgay*

Priceless life experiences have galvanized my personal and business achievements in a way that money never could. My hard-knock, high-stakes education helped me build and maintain habits of pure hustle, persuasion, salesmanship, and the ability to close.

Here's a story from my young life that illustrates an aspect of my personal growth.

Ruben Sanchez and Oscar Garcia were my two best childhood friends growing up in North Long Beach. We went all the way through elementary and middle school together and spent all of our time after school getting in and out of various scrapes. Ruben had a great heart but was one of the toughest guys I have ever met. He never backed down from a fight, no matter the odds—and he never lost one either. Oscar was more like me—a little more gentle and subdued, though neither of us liked to back down either, and we took our lumps sometimes. The two of us considered ourselves fortunate to have Ruben at our backs.

Ruben, Oscar, and I dug a hole underneath the chain-link fence in the back corner of the school playground, so we could come and go at will. While one of us stood guard, the other two would crawl under one at a time; then number three would shimmy under, and we were free! Sometimes we got away clean; often we did not. The punishment for leaving campus at lunch was either detention or suspension, depending on the mood of the official who caught us. The three of us endured our fair share of both punishments, but that didn't dampen our desire to push our boundaries wherever we could.

Most of our mischief began on a dare—we loved to challenge one another to take chances. There was a walkway that led from one part of the school to the other, with iron railings along both of its sides. One day, Ruben and Oscar challenged me to try and stick my head through the vertical bars holding up the railings. Of course, I rose to the challenge and squeezed my head right through the opening. Easy! The problem was—getting it back out. Try as I might, I was stuck. Milton, the school janitor, had to pry the bars apart to liberate me as my two friends laughed themselves silly and a teacher stood by to haul me to the principal's office to face my fate. We talked about that one for years.

> *Whatever it is you want out of life, go after it.*
> *Don't allow yourself to be a victim of fear.*
> —*Paul D. Forgay*

My family moved when I was in ninth grade, and I was enrolled in a new school, but I stayed in touch with my buddies throughout high school. As kids do, we eventually lost touch, but I found out later that Oscar died of an overdose behind the Dairy Queen, right across the street from our middle school. Ruben ended up doing some time in prison. I ran into him years later and never even asked him about it; I was just so damn happy to see him. If I had to guess, I'd say that it was probably because Ruben never backed down.

> *Everything you've ever wanted is*
> *on the other side of fear.*
> —*George Addair*

So why am I telling you stories of my stormy childhood in a book that is supposed to inspire you to be your best? Because I learned a lot from Ruben and Oscar, and it wasn't all by negative example. From these spirited, brave young men, I learned what a real friend truly is. I learned the genuine value of having people in your life who urge you to have confidence in yourself and do things you never thought you could do (even if those things are misguided sometimes). I learned what it means to attract and hold on to people who have your back no matter what.

While it's true that we all have many more acquaintances in life than true friends, in this regard, it is *quality* rather than *quantity* that counts. Find even one friend with the heart of a giant and the bravery of a lion who would fight for you if necessary and patch up your wounds when you fight for yourself, and you will never be destitute. You may be your own greatest asset—but a true friend is GOLDEN!

> *Leave no room for fear, for fear is a choice.*
> —*Paul D. Forgay*

My own priceless life experiences have galvanized me in business and in my personal life. My hard-knock, high-stakes education taught me to build and maintain the habits of pure hustle, persuasion, and salesmanship, but those things alone would never have led to success and happiness. I have also had to learn to listen to the needs of others, empathize, and respond in heartfelt and creative ways. Helping others attain their goals—whether they are my clients, my family, friends, or *you*, my readers—these things are as much a building block of success as my grit, perseverance, and tenacious work ethic. It's been my experience that difficult situations have a way of revealing a grateful heart and who you are as a person.

I feel like every day is a new beginning and that I will get better over time as long as I took control of my life with a sense of gratitude. I choose to grow and take responsibility for my actions. What I learned was one of the only ways I would be able to grow was through the daily personal development and being able to narrow my focus and work on shattering every one of my fears.

I decided to shatter my fears by clearing the chaos, clutter, ambiguity, extreme episodes of mayhem, and intense emotional states that resided within me and encircled my mindset. It's an awesome feeling to shatter one's own fears with the confidence and courage to turn adversity into opportunity, to turn sheer existence into a life of purpose. I hope my own "rich" life experiences will help you tap into the magic of knowing, deep down, that *you are your greatest asset.*

When I began to nurture my personal *SKILLS, HABITS, ATTITUDE*, my intellect and character became my shadow!

TURN PAIN INTO TRIUMPH ~ ADVERSITY INTO OPPORTUNITY!

SELF-AFFIRMATION
"I don't need attention and I don't need praise; my work ethic defines me and that's all I need."

HABITS
Get up every day between 2 AM and 3 AM without an alarm clock! Relentless work ethic!

SKILLS
Salesmanship; earning one's confidence, unique sales skills, and professional closer!

ATTITUDE
Chose to turn adversity into opportunity! Humility— stay humble!

Well, I am certainly wiser than this man. It is only too likely that neither of us has any knowledge to boast of; but he thinks that he knows something which he does not know, whereas I am quite conscious of my ignorance. At any rate, it seems that I am wiser than he is to this small extent, that I do not think that I know what I do not know.
—Socrates

Abolish the vultures of fear.
—Paul D. Forgay

CHAPTER 4

COURAGE

Pure courage and greatness occur amid
difficult times and struggles.
—*Paul D. Forgay*

Have the courage to stand your ground in the
midst of adversity, and you will fear nothing.
—*Paul D. Forgay*

W hen adversity strikes, my courage kicks in. One of life's greatest treasures is having the courage to turn failure in to victory. I believe in treating every day as a new beginning. By doing so, I began to summon the courage to take my life back. I started to feel a real sense of gratitude, which in turn gave me strength in treating every single day as a new beginning.

Courage is being able to find
order in times of chaos.
—*Paul D. Forgay*

"Be strong and
courageous, for
the Lord your God
is with you where
ever you Go."

Joshua 1:9

Dad,
I know you've been
having a hard time lately.
So I just wanted to let
you know how much I
love you and that I will
always be here for you
and supporting you
every step of the way.
Always remember to
keep your head up.
Things will get better
with time. I believe
in you and I know that
we will get through
this together.
Love always,
Naomi

Note from Naomi (daughter)

Perhaps you already know this, but you'd be surprised how many people don't. Courage does not mean *having any fear* or even *conquering the fear you have*. Most people who have done courageous things have been scared stiff while doing them—but have mastered the ability to stay calm in the chaos. And, most important, they have summoned the courage to acknowledge their fear and *act in spite of it.*

In whatever arena of life one may meet the
challenge of courage, whatever may be the sacrifices
he faces if he follow his conscience—the loss of
his friends, his fortune, his contentment, even the
esteem of his fellow men—each man must decide
for himself the course he will follow. The stories
of past courage can define that ingredient—they
can teach, they can offer hope, they provide
inspiration. But they cannot supply courage itself.
For this each man must look into his own soul.
—John F. Kennedy

The word courage comes from a Latin root word meaning "of the heart." Overtime, this meaning has changed; and today, we naturally associate courage with brave and valiant acts. Courage can also be construed as forward motion in the presence of fear and is situated in your heart and not your mind. I've learned that courage is a necessary virtue when we choose to do good, particularly when that is most problematic. Courage most demands our respect, especially when it experiences risk without self-centered gain. It has also been my experience that genuine courage comes from putting *what you must do* ahead of *your fear of doing it*. And that includes having the courage to face what you must change about yourself and take the steps to achieve those changes. It takes courage to address things in our lives that we are ashamed of or don't have the fortitude to talk about. Being brave is something that can't be taught in a classroom or read from a book. It's something that inspires you to do the right thing at the right time without thinking about it. Fearlessness and bravery often go hand in hand because they involve taking action when it is difficult—even scary—to do so. Being courageous might involve sharing the feelings of discouragement, confronting the pessimist, skeptics, naysayers, leaving home at the age of seventeen with nothing but your clothes and never looking back, or taking on a task so daunting that it makes you cringe just thinking about it. Another thing that takes courage is forgiveness.

> *Believe in yourself and not some predetermined*
> *process that promises instant wealth and success.*
> *If you grant your creativity, passion, charisma,*
> *tenacious work ethic and continued personal*
> *growth to develop; towering success will follow.*
> *—Paul D. Forgay*

I've often had to be courageous in my life simply because there was no other option. I knew I had to exhibit courage or live out the rest of my life knowing that I hadn't mustered up the requisite strength and aptitude. I'm not sure if courage comes naturally or is just something we summon up on a whim or a dare, but I do know that when I am confronted with something that requires action, I respond instinctively. I pray, and then I attempt to do the right thing, regardless of the risk or uncertainty of the act.

It was a feat of courage for me to write and publish this book. By doing so, I know that I am running the risk of being ridiculed, laughed at, treated negatively, rejection, and conceivably being treated inferior. The truth is, I don't care—because the simple act of writing has set me free from the savagery of fear and set me on a clear path to realizing my dreams. It feels great to *be real* in the face of adversity. I believe what I am doing can make a difference in someone's life. I believe in myself and what I know I can accomplish. There was a time when I'd never have believed I had the courage even to begin such a task.

The courage to forgive those who hurt you the most, the feeling of helplessness that can catapult you into the depth of the unknown—these are familiar feelings to me. Being scolded in front of others can be humiliating and shameful, and being beaten is even more demeaning. It can put you in a dark and lonely place, physically and mentally.

> *You cannot change the past; conversely, you*
> *can empower yourself to define your future.*
> *—Paul D. Forgay*

> *Compromising your core values*
> *exposes your weaknesses.*
> *—Paul D. Forgay*

I'll never forget the beatings I suffered—pants down, leaning against the bed with my knees and hands, pressed against the mattress to hold myself up. The moment the beating began, I started crying. I cried so much that after a while my tears ran dry. "Please stop!" I cried, but the beating did not stop. I began to pray that it would stop, to no avail. Finally, I'd fall facedown on the bed, reaching back with my hands, palms up, in the hope of preventing the pain from the lashing of the thick, wide black leather belt on my exposed backside. I can remember lying on the bed lifeless, looking over my right shoulder and wondering how someone could inflict so much pain on a child.

As much as I have wanted to forget those beatings, I am glad I never have. They are a constant reminder of the person I never want to be. I promised myself long ago that I would never lay a hand on my kids, and I haven't. Honestly? I am no longer mad about those beatings. I am thankful that God gave me the strength to forgive. Forgiveness and prayer have given me the faith and will to avoid the eerie, chilling unknown.

> *I endured and prevailed over my hardships*
> *with courage, determination, faith, prayer,*
> *and humility, to realize my true potential.*
> —*Paul D. Forgay*

Growing up in a family with no formal education made it that much more difficult for me to excel in school, let alone graduate. I managed to squeak through high school with a 2.2 GPA which I thought was generous, not because I was too stupid to do better but because I dedicated myself to the one thing—the only thing—I knew I was great at work. I worked day and night, relentlessly!

I say that I wasn't unintelligent, and you can probably tell that's true—but it's amazing that I figured that out because I never had any support or encouragement to better myself academically, I was on my own. I was told on numerous occasions by my family, friends, and peers that college was not for me. I will never forget the day my high school guidance counselor told me that I was lucky to be graduating at all. His advice was to get a job—any job I could. It has always been my understanding that the objective of a high school guidance counselor is to give some positive guidance, inspire, help identify my potential calling in life, and learning how to connect with others. This was far from the experience I had with my high school guidance counselor.

I remember that day as if it was yesterday because it changed me. Mr. Smith was sitting in his office with his feet up on his desk, leaning back with his hands clasped behind his head. From that position, he would spew out his so-called *guidance*, and his advice to me was, essentially, "Settle for anything you can get, Paul. You won't add an abundant amount of value to any workplace." It was at that moment that I summoned up my belief in myself. If no one else was going to believe in me, I'd have to find my sense of purpose on my own—and I knew I had infinitely more potential than that clown of a guidance counselor saw when he looked at me. His vision was limited, but mine was not. I was not going to allow him or anyone else to stand in the way of my leading a purposeful life.

> *Courage, therefore, is the power of the mind to overcome fear...fear has a definite object which may be faced, analyzed, attacked, and, if need be, endured...*
> *Courage and cowardice are antithetical. Courage is an inner resolution to go forward in spite of obstacles and frightening situations; cowardice is a submissive surrender to circumstance. Courage breeds creative self-affirmation; cowardice produces destructive self-abnegation. Courage faces fear and thereby masters it; cowardice represses fear and is thereby mastered by it. Courageous men never lose the zest for living even though their life situation is zestless; cowardly men, overwhelmed by the uncertainties of life, lose the will to live. We must constantly build dikes of courage to hold back the flood of fear.*
> *—Martin Luther King Jr.*

> *It takes courage to show yourself. It takes courage to create and share. It takes courage to speak your mind. It takes courage to be honest with yourself. It takes courage to face the realization that your fear may be rooted in jealousy or insecurity. But the other choice is cowardice, and that is not a choice at all.*
> *—Martin Luther King Jr.*

As I had done before and have done since, I decided to turn adversity into opportunity. The high school I attended had a kind of competition every year. It was supposed to be a gauge of accomplishment in various areas, but what it really measured was who the most popular guy in school was. To compete, you had to be sponsored by one of the campus clubs. There ended up being over a dozen guys in the contest.

At the time, I was dating Lisa, a beautiful, kind, and caring girl who happened to be involved in one of the girls' clubs. She asked me if I would represent her club in the competition, catching me completely off guard. Did I have what it took to compete? The idea made me pretty nervous—but I summoned up my courage and said *yes.*

The competition comprised three categories, and I quickly took inventory of how I thought I might stack up. The first category was physique, and I knew I'd do fine there. I'd been working out since the age of twelve and was proud of the results. The second category was talent, and that was a little trickier. I didn't have a conventional "talent"—didn't play an instrument or do magic—so I'd have to be a little creative in that area. I decided to lip sync and dance, neither of which I was very good at. I loved R&B music growing up and still do. I picked a song by the Manhattans: "Shining Star." Every chance I got, I would pop the tape into my boom box and crank it up, memorizing every word and inflection and pairing it with my best moves. I practiced constantly until I had my routine down pat. I still remember every word and gesture and could perform it today if somebody put on that song.

The final category in the competition was off-the-cuff speaking. The host would randomly select a question for each contestant, and we'd have a short time to answer it. I don't remember the question I was asked, but I do remember feeling more nervous about this part than either of the others. I had never spoken in front of people before, certainly not three hundred of my peers and teachers! But I sucked it up and found the courage to get it done. It helped that Lisa was sitting towards the front of the auditorium with a giant poster with my name on it, yelling out words of encouragement.

When the judges narrowed down the field to the finalist, I was one of them. Before I could get over my surprise, they announced the winner: it wasn't me. Out of eighteen original contestants, I ended up being one of the finalists!

I can't begin to tell you how much I learned from that experience—mainly about myself. I learned that if I just have the courage to step up and try something, I might excel at it. I might even prevail and be the *best* at it. I may have only been one of the finalists in that contest, but I'd never felt more like a winner in my life. That is the kind of courage I have tried to put into practice every day since. And whenever I hear the Manhattans sing, "Oooh yeah, honey, you are my shining star…," I mentally change the lyrics to, "Oooh yeah, honey, *I am my own* shining star!"

I have never been accused of being "normal," and I would never want to be! I know that I am unique, with unique resources, and these resources, along with my unwavering faith in God, have always empowered me to take risks. It has been my experience as an entrepreneur that taking specific calculated risks certainly outweigh reckless and thoughtless risks. I am a true believer in taking calculated risks. By doing so, I have been ridiculed, laughed at, been and called a stupid fool—a fool of fools. Usually by those who choose to work in a box, live the nine to five grind, and report to a belligerent supervisor, sitting in traffic for hours, lack of freedom and building someone else's dream and not yours. Risk-taking teaches you more about yourself, demonstrates confidence, and creates change. To accomplish your goals and dreams, it is important to learn from the calculated risks you take.

Risk-taking requires a strong foundation, and mine (and I hope yours) is built on these eight pillars of strength:

- Courage
- Faith
- Gratitude
- Heart
- Humility
- Hustle
- Prayer
- Relentless Work Ethic

It is these rock-solid building blocks that have given me the strength to overcome hardship and forge my own pathway to success.

I found courage in fighting my way back from frequent episodes in dealing with my personal adverse situations. Finding the courage to fight back against all my personal ill-fated circumstances has shown me what an insane work ethic, perseverance, positive and insightful attitude, respect, and the habits of a natural-born hustler has to offer in abundance. I believe everyone has the courage to fight back. I urge you to fight back against your personal adverse situations, pessimists and naysayers and you too will experience what it feels like when true courage kicks in!

Courage is based on the habits of your heart.
—Paul D. Forgay

Embracing my self-confidence have given me the
courage to work through the darkness of negativity,
adversity, naysayers, pain, and depth of despair.
—Paul D. Forgay

CHAPTER 5

MY HERO

Gratitude is a great indicator
of a persons character.
—Paul D. Forgay

Don't mistake humility, gratitude
or kindness for weakness
—Paul D. Forgay

I believe a hero is someone who makes a positive impact on you or contributes something positive to the world. Heroes do not expect compensation for their generosity, knowledge, leadership, or guidance. Heroic deeds don't go unnoticed, especially when the hero is someone you've met on this magnificent journey called life. The awesome thing about discovering your hero is the realization that there are heroes among us.

I've encountered many people in my life, but heroes are few and far between. They seem to appear magically in your life when the timing is right and can influence you in powerful, positive, but subtle ways that you'll never forget. I am blessed to have met a genuine hero.

I was introduced to Coach in the winter of 1983, on a day I didn't realize would change my life forever. I had just returned home from boot camp and military occupational specialty training. My friends from high school were attending Long Beach City College, and they encouraged me to sign up for classes too. I eventually enrolled and was introduced to the men's club advisor Mr. Phillip Q. Shrotman—a.k.a. Coach—who was also a business professor. I attended his classes, learned a lot, and had a blast listening to his jokes and appreciating his swift wit. I ended up joining the men's club (my friends were already members). Coach struck a chord with me right away, and on top of that, his daughter, Lori, was without a doubt one of the prettiest, kindest, and most loving people I had ever met. I fell in love with her the first time I laid eyes on her. I was blessed enough to have discovered my hero, but I had come upon a lady who was lively, tender, intelligent, passionate, courageous, elegant and incredibly striking!

> *Experience affords you the ability to transform*
> *adverse circumstances into opportunity.*
> —*Paul D. Forgay*

> *Compromising your core values*
> *exposes your weaknesses.*
> —*Paul D. Forgay*

Coach was, is, and will always be the only man that I consider my perfect role model, friend, mentor, and father figure. He is the hero I had always hoped for. He taught me what it means to be a man, father, and successful businessman without my even realizing it. To this day, he's a one-of-a-kind character: intelligent, funny, and a great father and husband—and the finest businessman I've ever met. His wife, whom he kiddingly refers to as "Mrs. What's-Her-Face," is stunning, loving, and the classiest lady I know. How she has put up with Coach's shenanigans for over fifty years is beyond my comprehension.

Kidding aside, I know without a doubt that he adores her and would lay down his life for her. Coach, Mrs. Shrotman, and Lori have shown me what it means to be truly loved, through the good times and the bad times. When I broke my ankle trying out for the Long Beach

City College football team, they took me into their home, cared for me physically and emotionally, fed me, gave me a place to sleep, and loved me. I think Coach would disagree—or at least joke about the emotional part. Every Thursday night, we would have popcorn and watch the show *Cheers*. As simple as it may sound, those Thursday nights are some of the fondest memories of my life. While they may not have recognized it at the time, I was living a dream. One of the biggest regrets of my life was not furthering my relationship with Lori. Even after she and I stopped dating, Mr. and Mrs. Shrotman treated me with love, which is one of the many reasons why I love, respect, and admire them.

> *Charisma, passion and a clear*
> *vision drive positive thoughts.*
> —*Paul D. Forgay*

Coach was my single biggest inspiration and the reason I attended and graduated from Chapman University. He has taught me many things throughout my life, including what it takes to become a great salesperson, businessman, negotiator, and leader, all while being crafty and witty. I realize that his success has come from being each of these, and he has always had an uncanny way of making the pursuit of these qualities fun and serious at the same time.

He also taught me that talent is not everything, champions show up, and if you intend on taking advantage of people, you will end up losing. Coach, without even knowing it devoted portions of his life to the contribution that he served something greater than himself.

> *The pinnacle of success is being able to reach*
> *out and help the less-fortunate, so reach out!*
> —*Paul D. Forgay*

It would be impossible to thank Coach and Mrs. Shrotman enough for everything they have done for me, but one of the greatest delights of my life has been introducing my kids to them and watching those children come to love and admire them as I do. When my kids first got to know Coach, he would always greet them by saying,

"YELLOW!" They were young at the time, so they didn't really understand what he was saying. I explained to them that it was his funny way of saying *hello*. To this day, he greets them with a big "yellow," but now he gets three loud *yellows* in return.

Lori passed away of breast cancer several years after meeting my children, and that was without question one of the most heartbreaking days of my life. I have very few regrets, but not furthering our relationship is certainly at the top of the list. I loved her and miss her dearly!

There's a song by Keith Urban called "Thank You." Several of the verses in this song struck a chord with me. Without "Coach" wisdom, guidance, and friendship, I wouldn't have seen the morning sun.

I will always respect, love, and admire Coach for being a great friend, mentor, and father figure. As I said—he is my hero. I hope you find yours.

EXPERIENCE IS THE BEST TEACHER
"The great Roman leader Julius Caesar recorded the earliest known version of this proverb, 'Experience is the teacher of all things,' in 'De Bello Civili' (c. 52 BC).

A natural-born hustler is somewhat of a
phenomenon; humble, yet relentless with
the unrivaled desire to succeed even in
the smallest of arenas. I natural-born
hustler is nothing less than a phenom.
—Paul D. Forgay

Chapter 6

Humility and Mistakes

*Humility is the hidden gem behind
long-term success and greatness.*
                    —*Paul D. Forgay*

I've made and lost a lot of money in my life. Coming from nothing, working until I had everything I've ever dreamed of, losing it, then gaining it again has been one of the most humbling experiences of my life, PERIOD. You see, when I had an abundance of money, I had a lot of friends—or so-called friends. Most of them became less than acquaintances once I lost everything. It's unfortunate, but the people you help out in their hour of need are likely to forget you when you have nothing of material value to give.

But being humbled by these experiences was not necessarily a bad thing. Humility—being able to accept a variety of outcomes without bitterness or resentment—has come to play a significant role in my life. Being humbled has made me a more understanding person who can accept situations I was not accustomed to without outrage or embarrassment. It has helped me better understand my own strengths and weaknesses, morally and otherwise.

*Do not allow your ego or self-centered
ways to stymie the virtue of humility.*
                    —*Paul D. Forgay*

44

I remember the day I was turned away from the home I lived in with my family. I don't only remember it; it will be etched in my mind forever. It was humbling, to say the least. Earlier that day, I was at football practice at Long Beach City College. During practice, I broke my ankle while doing tip drills. A friend took me to the hospital, where they proceeded to insert a long needle into my ankle, which by that time was the size of a large softball; it was uncomfortable and a bit painful. By the time I left the hospital, it was a dark out and raining heavily. A friend dropped me off at my house. I had a cast up to my knee and was only able to get around by using the crutches I was given. I knocked on the door several times, and it finally opened. The person on the other side of the door was far from understanding; they yelled at me to get out of here and slammed the door in my face. People can deny things, refuse to take accountability for their actions, blaming others, I know the truth because I was the person that the door was slammed on. It was demeaning and sad at the same time. I felt like I was being punished for something—something I never did. I was the one who was paying the price for someone else's unhappiness. I got into my 1964 VW Square Back that I paid seven hundred dollars for and drove away.

1964 VW Square Back

Believe me when I tell you that wasn't an easy task. My car was a stick shift. I ended up sleeping in my car for several weeks, but I learned a lot. I learned I had to move my car every few hours so the police would not fine me or arrest me for loitering. This was not the first time I slept in my car for days at a time and certainly would not be the last time. I was too embarrassed to share this with family or friends, so I have kept it to myself up until this very moment. I learned that sometimes you're the person who is chastised for someone else's lack of happiness bitterness and resentfulness that night, I promised myself that I would never be the person on the other side of that door!

Humility has given me the dexterity necessary
to weed out the weak, naysayers, negative
people and adverse circumstances in my life.
—Paul D. Forgay

Difficult times have helped me in living a life of grateful humility. A gift that can only become possible through personal hardships, life lessons, and accepting of a modest view of one's own importance, humility is one of the life's great equalizers and one of life's best defenses—and it first takes root in your heart. A proud person forced to be humble has become enlightened. He welcomes his challenges. In my case, I gained an altered view of my own importance in the world—and that was not a bad thing. It made me appreciate what I had and let go of what I don't need in order to live a purposeful life. People choose to conveniently forget or take accountability for things they've done to you, but I will never forget, but I do forgive, just as I would pray that others forgive me for the mistakes I've made.

My rich life experiences have shown me that deep down inside of all of us, there's a beautiful radiant light, a graceful light that has the power to no longer fear darkness. This power will liberate your soul; it has mine. There's a song by Tim McGraw called "Humble and Kind" that offers inspiration to me. It's more gratifying and easier to help the next one in line, **ALWAYS STAY HUMBLE AND KIND!**

How you deal with adversity can be the
deciding factor between success and failure.
—Paul D. Forgay

Life mistakes happen; this is how we learn and how we grow as a person. I pray that God gives me the strength to bounce back and forgive me for my mistakes and helps me to live a more purposeful, authentic life and be of service to others. When I was eleven years old, I was on our school's flag football team. I was a decent player, and I loved the game, but I was missing that competitive edge that comes from wearing football cleats. At the time, Puma cleats were the ones to have; you weren't considered cool without them. I wanted to be good at the game and cool too, so I wanted those cleats desperately. I worked and worked and finally made enough money to buy a pair.

8th Football

FRONT (L to R): R. Peoples, D. Erickson, T. Holden, E. Flores, P. Forgay. REAR: T. Greene, O. Mendez, W. Robinson, B. Oden, G. Calhoun, E. James, P. Alvarez, A. Saglietto, Coach Allen.

Jefferson Junior High Football Team

I was so excited to show off my new cleats! I remember tying the shoelaces together so I could hang them on the handlebars of my bike. As I rode to school with the cleats on full display, I decided I needed one more thing to make my day complete: a pack of Bubblicious bubblegum. I decided to stop at one of the many liquor stores that I passed on my way to school, grab a pack of the gum, jump on my bike, and speed off. But my little crime spree didn't go so well. A guy delivering soda saw me lift the gum and tipped off the man behind the register. As I ran out of the store, I could hear him say, "Hey, that kid just put something in his pocket!"

The man at the checkout let out a yell and began to chase me. I jumped on my bike and rode so fast that my brand-new Pumas— which I had proudly bought with my own hard-earned money—flew off my handlebars and landed in the street. There was no way I could retrieve them without getting caught, so I just sped away. I had a pack of gum, but no Puma cleats. I learned the hard way that most of my toughest lessons in my life came from my greatest mistakes!

In the absence of humility; uncertainty
disturbs peace of mind.
—*Paul D. Forgay*

You could say I "got away with" my bad deed, but I really didn't because it has troubled me to this day. I learned a big lesson about stealing, though: it's wrong, and it's not worth it. I didn't become a better player that day, but I did become a better person.

Wisdom can't be taught; it's
something acquired over time.
—*Paul D. Forgay*

CHAPTER 7

TIME

Worrying is the thief of time.
—*Paul D. Forgay*

We have become pawns in the hands of time.
—*Paul D. Forgay*

Time is one of the only things in life that's truly out of our control. It's been said that if it's worth doing, it's worth doing right, and I agree. Take the time to do things right. Utilize your imagination and creativity, and be different from everyone else! Doing it right doesn't limit you to the basics or the tried-and-true. If you tap into your *Skills, Habits and Attitude*, you will go beyond just being right to being extraordinarily great.

It was especially important for me to write about the stigma that is unjustly associated with mental illness. The media spends most of its time and assets to prey on such negative stories; murder, robberies, war, anything that will sell, just in the name of increased revenue and ratings. The better the ratings, the better time slot, which means potentially increasing their revenue significantly. Time does matter in every aspect of our lives. Instead of the massive amount garbage that is played relentlessly every day on the TV, radio, and social media. Media platforms should pay more attention to the advocates for all just causes, educate themselves, spend time listening and working toward improving the lives of others; this may or may not increase revenue or ratings, but it will save lives.

In 2019 there was an incident in Southern California where an active duty police officer confessed that he was not shot at from some apartment buildings close to the station as he earlier said.

"There was no sniper, no shots fired, and no gunshot injury sustained to his shoulder. "(It was) completely fabricated" (Supervisor).

The local community leader organized a press conference soon after the shooting and said it was risky to house people with mental illness across the street from a police station.

Numerous residents voiced uneasiness about the comments made by the local community leader in the outcome of this incident and the challenging impact those comments may possibly have on the local mentally impaired population.

Once again, the media and others rushed to judgment in no time. The media intends to create chaos and instilling the propaganda of fear; unfortunately, fear sells.

Time never stops ticking; it is a constant reminder that every second counts.

Do not allow people to waste your time. There is an old saying that time is money, and that is true, but it is also true that money cannot buy time. Everyone has the same twenty-four hours in a day!

> *The two most powerful warriors are patience*
> *and time…so remember: great achievements*
> *do take time, there is no overnight success.*
> —*Leo Tolstoy*

Maximizing the use of my time has become a habit. The older I get, the more meaningful and precious time has become. I think about all the things I have accomplished and the things I still dream of doing, and time seems to fly by uncontrollably. The tyranny of time never misses a beat, not for a second.

Having the self-discipline and self-confidence to recognize growth in times of pain and struggle makes for a solid foundation during times of adverse circumstances. I know people with extreme intellect, but that will only get you so far in life. Self-confidence, hard work, persistence, pure hustle, a tenacious work ethic, and proper timing have the power to thrust you through the most turbulent of times.

Above Perad's still-life portrayal

Perad's still-life and portrayal painting depicts several representations of the passage of time, including a clock, an hourglass, old photographs, a blown-out candle, skulls, and globe—a nod to the very literal burning of the world.
—Antonio de Pereda
Allegory of Vanity
(c1632–1636)–Giclee

In business and in life, you will experience plenty of setbacks; and at times, excruciating failures. The question is, Do you have what it takes to make a comeback and be even better than you were? Are you strong enough to rebound from devastating circumstances? Resiliency is a great indicator; being resilient can also mean sticking up for someone or something when others disagree, refusing to back down and then, if you do get knocked down, having enough strength, determination and mental toughness to get back up.

I am more aware of my actions, feelings, motivations, wants, and needs than ever before. I'm making a conscious effort to filter the things I say and do. It's hard sometimes, but I know this helps me make more informed decisions and an even better person. It also gives me the confidence I need to be me and not someone others want me to be.

> *Success is not about being average. It's*
> *about choosing to be extraordinary.*
> —*Paul D. Forgay*

As if it were yesterday, I remember playing with a set of plastic cowboys and Indians I received for Christmas one year. The game came in a box approximately 18×24 inches and included all the little figures, plus plastic horses, teepees, and a fort. I was so happy when I opened that box! I remember lying on my stomach on the front porch, playing with it by myself for hours. I could not have been more content or worry-free. My, how time flies.

I've learned over the years that time doesn't care if you're sitting, standing, driving, or walking; it just keeps passing by. If you allow it, time can be the nemesis of your soul and the thief of your dreams. Don't let others waste your time with nonsense and trivial things. Get down to business and make every second count. As a seasoned salesperson, I understand that, occasionally, time is not on my side, so I try my best to sift through the deals in front of me and discard anything I feel isn't worthy of my time. I do the same in my personal life, and so should you.

I'm not trying to be egotistical when I talk about all that I've accomplished, because I have also failed on more than a few occasions. I think candor is the best course of action in any situation— being truthful with yourself and with others—and that is how I conduct every aspect of my life. I think you would be surprised by how many people you know would appreciate hearing the truth up front, rather than having their time wasted while you skirt around it. Nobody wants their time wasted; and lying, fibbing, softening the truth, or hedging your bets are a waste of your time and theirs.

It's a fine line sometimes—especially in business—because the people you are dealing with may not recognize their need for what you have to offer. They may think you're wasting their time just by presenting it to them, but if you've done your research and what you say is true, it's much easier to bring them around to your point of view. If you present your case rationally, honestly, and succinctly—and if you've chosen a client who is not a waste of your time—you will soon convince them that your product and or service is of benefit to their company and their bottom line. Now, do you see how making the most of your time can benefit you in business, as well as in life?

Yes, time does fly by, so make the most of it because that last second is gone forever!

Father Time plays no favorites.
—Paul D. Forgay

Champions work relentlessly, produce results,
show up every day and get things done.
—Paul D. Forgay

CHAPTER 8

IT'S ABOUT HEART

*I have no special talent to speak of; I am a
work in progress; failure, hardships, rewards,
success, and rich life experiences. Each of
these has given me the fortitude and tenacity
TO TURN PAIN INTO TRIUMPH—
ADVERSITY INTO OPPORTUNITY.*
—Paul D. Forgay

*I can overcome anything because I possess
something money can't buy, heart.*
—Paul D. Forgay

If there's one word that describes what I am made of, it would have to be *heart*. I was poor, but I was rich because I have a dream and a deep-rooted desire to be the person I know I can be. I am the only one who knows what I am capable of. You can be a genius, incredibly skilled at what you do, but I've learned that without heart, tenacious work ethic and the ability to survive diminish considerably. At times, my mind looks for what is wrong, but my heart will always look for what is true.

*"Most men lead lives of quiet desperation and
go to the grave with the song still in them."*
—Henry David Thoreau

54

I developed the mind-set that I could overcome anything by having *heart*. I've learned that it is what has allowed me to move forward when times were tough and quitting would have been much easier. If I were to quit or just get by, I don't think I would respect my own efforts, and that would mean I couldn't respect myself.

I was not born with a silver spoon in my mouth or shoes made of gold, but I was born with the heart of a giant—and that trumps silver and gold. Precious metals can be bought, but the heart of a giant is not for sale.

Sketch of Paul

Do what you love, work hard,
exemplify conviction, stay humble
and always listen to your heart.
—*Paul D. Forgay*

Having heart can be a little difficult to explain to someone who has never had to depend on their heart to get them through unforeseen adversities. Your heart pumps blood through your body to keep you alive, but it also contains the fire and drives beyond what you know you possess. Having heart is not the same as being persistent or determined; it's more like a combination of courage and fortitude. It is what makes it possible for you not only to go that extra mile but to do it in record time without hesitation.

I believe that the concept of *heart* can be traced back before the Common Era, to the time of David and Goliath. David was the much smaller man and was thought to have no chance of prevailing against the mighty Goliath—or even surviving. Yet, as you know, he conquered his giant adversary armed only with a sling shot and five stones while Goliath possessed a staff and a javelin. How did he do that? With faith and heart in abundance.

Whenever I feel like quitting or not giving something my all, I take a moment to summon up my own belief in myself and my abilities. With faith, tenacious work ethic and heart, I forge ahead. And I win.

> *"I have the heart of a giant and will not allow anyone or anything to defeat me—not even myself."*
> —*Paul D. Forgay*

> *"If my mind can conceive it, and my heart can believe it—then I can achieve it."*
> —*Muhammad Ali*

Persistence and determination have always played key roles in my life. When I was ten years old, nobody would hire me because of my age. But I needed money, so every weekend I loaded up my lawn mower with a rake, dustpan, plastic bags, hedge clippers, and broom. I knocked on every door until someone hired me to do yard work. Anyone who said no would get a return visit from me every weekend, until I was able to turn a no into a maybe and a maybe into a yes. I was persistent and determined and would not allow them to say no forever.

Because of my persistence, I ended up getting more work than I could handle and ended up hiring several friends to help me. For me, a *no* is never final—it's just the beginning. Without persistence and determination, I knew that I would always be average. I chose to be extraordinary. In my experience *Persistence and determination require never giving up, pressing on against all odds.* They are just as important as talent or skill, but they can't be taught; they must come from within and can be utilized in both your professional and personal life. Use them to become the best salesperson in your field or to earn enough money to live out your dreams. Sheer determination and persistence are essential as you strive to become the person and the professional you want to be. I experienced at a very young age that I am my greatest challenge, competing against myself and not the competition pushed me even harder.

Success is being able to do the simplest of tasks consistently, efficiently, professionally and with spirited passion.
—Paul D. Forgay

Persistence and determination are there when you wake up and when you go to sleep. If you live them day in and day out, they become part of you. There's something inside of you that says, *Yes, I can, and I will.* Don't give up, don't ever give up and don't ever give in to the annoying naysayers. My entire life has depended on using my sheer persistence and determination to help me achieve the goals and fulfill the expectations I set for myself. They have even aided me in navigating my failures.

When I was attending the local junior college, there was an athletic award given out every year for the best all-around IM athlete. To win it, you had to get the most points of anyone for running, swimming, weightlifting, biking, and other athletic endeavors. The competition played out over the entire school year.

I knew I could compete, but I wanted to win. This was in spite of the fact that I was carrying a full load of classes, working forty-plus hours a week, sharing an apartment with two roommates, and I didn't own a car. That's right—no car—but I did have a decent bike that got me where I needed to go when I couldn't bum a ride from a friend.

I knew I could win the award in spite of all those obstacles. And you know what? I did it. I won the award for best all-around

IM athlete. I received a fine-looking trophy, and my name was added to a plaque with past recipients. But for me, it was about more than just winning a trophy or seeing my name on a plaque. It was about achieving a goal I'd set for myself. Determination, persistence and Heart each played a huge part in my reaching that goal and proving to myself that I could do whatever I set out to do because I possess the heart of a giant.

Calvin Coolidge 30ᵗʰ President of The United States of America put it well:

> NOTHING IN THE WORLD CAN TAKE THE PLACE OF PERSISTENCE. TALENT WILL NOT; NOTHING IS MORE COMMON THAN UNSUCCESSFUL MEN/WOMEN OF TALENT. GENIUS WILL NOT... THE WORLD IS FULL OF EDUCATED DERELICTS. PERSISTENCE AND DETERMINATION ALONE ARE OMNIPOTENT. THE SLOGAN "PRESS ON" HAS SOLVED AND WILL ALWAYS SOLVE THE PROBLEMS OF THE HUMAN RACE.

> *A natural-born hustler learns to live*
> *above their circumstances.*
> *—Paul D. Forgay*

> *Being intellectually gifted does not guarantee*
> *success. You must possess a tenacious work*
> *ethic, determination, heart of a giant and the*
> *innate hunger of a natural born hustler.*
> *—Paul D. Forgay*

> *Carpe diem. Seize the day, boys.*
> *Make your lives extraordinary.*
> *—Robin Williams*

As a kid, I knew that I was never going to be the most intellectually gifted, biggest, or quickest, so I focused on the one thing I knew how to do: work. I worked relentlessly—and I still do. Throughout my journey I've been fortunate enough to have performed numerous types of jobs: I've mowed lawns, bused tables, scrubbed toilets, waited tables, cook, bouncer, security guard, forklift driver, warehouse worker, and truck driver. I've bagged groceries, swept and mopped floors, cleaned windows, pulled weeds, delivered groceries, coached, and volunteered. I've been a trainer, teacher's assistant, paperboy, professional salesperson, business consultant, sales strategist, motivational speaker—and that's just to name a few. These jobs have provided me with a lot of things beyond what a paycheck has to offer: humility, ambition, dreams, persistence, determination, gratitude—and all because of my insane and excessive work ethic. It's not as if I loved all these jobs, not at all, but I knew they were stepping-stones toward my ultimate goals and dream.

Once I'd made up my mind that my work ethic would define me, I never looked back. A strong work ethic is something to be proud of, but it is not easy to master. Anyone can demonstrate an exemplary work ethic for a short amount of time, but what sets me apart is that I have held on to it over the course of a lifetime, year in and year out.

It's not just about getting up on time or getting to work on time; it's about what you do and how you do it. It means working with passion, intensity, and pure grit. Most everyone has a work ethic, but some are stronger than others. I prefer to grind it out 24/7/365, which to some people is insane. Keep in mind that the ideas, dreams, and ambitions that many might have considered inconceivable have come from those thought to be insane. The advertising slogan "Just Do It" is, without a doubt, one of the greatest and well-known ever (bravo, Nike). You know why? Because it is great advice. If there's something you want to get done, harness your relentless work ethic and *just do it.*

I don't need attention, and I don't need praise.
My work ethic defines me, and that's all I need.
                                            —Paul D. Forgay

I know this for sure: I will never be outworked. You know why? Because my family depends on me. I have always outworked anyone, and I will go to my grave knowing that I gave everything I had.

As a child, I was taught to crawl first,
walk and then run. Becoming a successful
entrepreneur is not much different; except
crawling and walking are not in the equation.
—Paul D. Forgay

A relentless work ethic can be learned, but I believe I was born with it. *It's in my DNA.* There's a difference between working hard and working hard, smart, with heart and a rock-solid mind-set. I know I can outlast you. You will not outwork me! I never just compete; I dominate. I don't wear a watch, and I don't own a clock because my relentless work ethic doesn't care if it's 3:00 p.m. or 3:00 a.m. I know what I have to do without anyone telling me because I am a survivor. My work ethic speaks for me, so there's no need for me to sell myself. My value is encased in it: it's who I am, and it's what I do.

Persistence and self-determination will
enable you to push through what your
mind perceives your limits to be.
—Paul D. Forgay

One of my most important goals is to give it everything I have to whatever I do. Everything—and I mean everything—I've ever accomplished has been as a result of my work ethic. This is not something I think about doing; it is something I live every day. I've learned over time that my learning opportunities were limited by my willingness to be teachable.

Writing this book is a great example of something I've achieved against the odds. It's something I have always wanted to do, so I am *just doing it.*

If I didn't have a resolute work ethic, determination, courage, heart, and faith, you wouldn't be holding this book in your hand.

I wouldn't have been able to share with you all that I believe about the potential in each of us and how unleashing *your greatest asset* can change your life the way it changed mine. I was never one to follow the crowd; be different, but be responsible, be of service to others silence the naysayers, and write your own script.

Hitting rock bottom is an ugly, dark, dismal
and lonely place. Do I settle for a rock bottom
life, let it destroy me or do I reach deep within
my creative skills, imagination, soul, heart,
and champion what I am capable of.
—Paul D. Forgay

Professional salespeople do not allow themselves
to get caught up in the "next week" style of
doing business; next week is too late.
—Paul D. Forgay

CHAPTER 9

RESPECT

Never allow anyone to depreciate your self-worth.
—Paul D. Forgay

Quitting is just another way of demonstrating
that you don't respect your efforts or yourself.
—Paul D. Forgay

The area in which I grew up was the complete opposite of the setting for the long-running TV show *The Brady Bunch*. North Long Beach, California, was riddled with gangs, including the East Side Longos, the West Side Longos, the Bloods, the Crips, SWP (Supreme White Power), and SOS (Sons of Samoa). My first encounter with a gang member came when I was in sixth grade.

During recess, we would always play kickball. One day, as I took my usual spot at second base, another kid pushed me and announced that *he* would be playing the position. A good friend of mine who was much bigger than both of us told the kid to move aside and never bother me again. I didn't know it at the time, but the kid's older brother Jesse was affiliated with one of the aforementioned gangs. Had I known, I might have given up second base that day.

Strength and fortitude reveal themselves
most effective in times of struggle.
—Paul D. Forgay

I forgot all about the incident until one day, as my sibling and I walked to a friend's house, I noticed several kids zooming past us on bikes. When I say *several kids,* it was actually fourteen of them—and they weren't just kids; they were members of that gang. And one of them was Jesse. As they went by us, I heard one of them say my name. And in an instant, they all turned and came right at us. They hopped off their bikes and let them fall to the ground, then commenced pushing us, hitting us, and kicking us. Jesse himself swung from a tree and kicked me as hard as he could right in the face. We tried to fight back, but we were so outnumbered that we took what my father would refer to as an ass-whooping.

By the time the gang kids left, I had bruises everywhere, swollen lips, and blood all over my torn clothes. One of the many things I learned that day—and from growing up in North Long Beach in general—is that you have to stand up for yourself, even in difficult situations. It's been my personal experience that if you don't stand up for yourself, or if you show fear of any kind, the abuse will be compounded. I learned several years later that Jesse had gone to prison and wasn't getting out anytime soon. As for me, I was driving nice cars and living in a beautiful home. Sometimes adversity can be a character builder, humbling you and making you that much more determined to be the person you desire to be. Paul the Apostle—1 Thessalonians 4:11–12:

> And to make it your ambition to lead a quiet life:
> You should mind your own business and work
> with your hands, just as we told you, so that your
> daily life may win the *respect* of outsiders and
> so that you will not be dependent on anybody.
> (New International Version, NIV)

*Where you come from will play a significant
role in who you are, but you're the only
one who chooses where you want to go
and how you want to get there.*
—Paul D. Forgay

As a young boy I had plenty of friends growing up who were affiliated with one gang or another. In those days, there was one thing that everyone sought, and it wasn't money or fancy cars: it was *respect*. Respect isn't something you're born with; it is something you earn—and sometimes you have to figure that out the hard way. Respect others no matter who they are or where they're from. If you respect them, you can earn their respect in return. And that can keep you from a world of trouble. This is one of the many life experiences that made me the person I am today.

> *I was able to grind through my hardships*
> *because I knew that I was special and*
> *had a specific purpose in life; I recognized*
> *one day was going to be my day.*
> —*Paul D. Forgay*

I have been ridiculed, laughed at, and called a stupid fool—a fool of fools. Generally, by those who choose to work in a box, live the nine-to-five grind, and report to a aggressive manager, sitting in traffic for hours, absence of freedom. Calculated risk-taking teaches you more about yourself, demonstrates confidence, and creates change. To achieve your goals and dreams, it's important to learn from the calculated risks you take.

Paul—giving presentation

It has always been a dream of mine to go to college; my strategy was to go into the military after I graduated from high school, so I enlisted soon after graduating. I wanted to be the first in my family to graduate from college. The plan was to send all my checks home; my parents would save the money, so when I got back, I would have enough money to at least start working toward my dream of graduating from college.

I worked twenty-four-seven for a solid eight months straight—the whole time I was sending my checks home. I will never forget the day I came home from Basic Training and Military Occupational Skill Training. I remember walking through the front door of my parents' house. It was a strange feeling still quiet. My biological father was sitting in the same brown recliner he had for years. It was bizarre because neither of my parents even got up to welcome me home. You could feel the tension! I remember my parents telling me that all the money I sent home was gone. It was simply weird; I was not mad at them. I was beyond hurt; I was devastated. The sad part is they began to point fingers at one another as if it was only one person's fault. That did not matter to me who did what. That was the day I lost what little respect I had left for them. I forgave them right on the spot. That did not help the fact that my respect for them disintegrated right before my eyes. It was about respect—the respect I lost for them on that very day.

During the times of uncertainty, I discovered something about myself that I did not know that I would be able to forgive. What I learned was, although I would forgive, I did not have to be around them or even like them; this was my choice. You will experience a lot of pain, adversity, defeats, and failure; but you must not quit. I also learned that all of us need to look out for the dream takers—these are the individuals that will attempt to steal your money and your dreams every single day of your life just like that day I walked into my parents' house. I was not going to let anything or anyone steal my dreams, including the so-called family!

It is these rock-solid building blocks that have given me the strength to overcome hardship and forge my own pathway to success.

- Courage
- Faith
- Gratitude
- Heart
- Humility
- Hustle
- Prayer
- Relentless Work Ethic

In quietness and in confidence
shall be your strength.
—*Isaiah, 30:15*

Success and respect are earned, not given.
—*Paul D. Forgay*

I have not always worked *for* myself, but I am always working *on* myself—physically, mentally, and spiritually. I am always feeding my mind with positive thoughts, such as the following:

Life can be like a roller coaster. Sometimes you're up, and sometimes you're down. *Being down* can mean that you're depressed, broke, struggling with life's day-to-day challenges or just temporarily down on your luck. On the flip side, *being up* can mean that you're doing well financially, enjoying a rich family life, and feeling stress-free, happy, and comfortable. No matter which direction your roller coaster is headed, it's important to remember that it will change because change is inevitable. It will go the other way.

The thing to focus on when you're *up* is, *What can I do to hold on to what I have, safeguard and enjoy it, be of service to others and build on it for the future?*

The thing to focus on when you're *down* is, being of service to others. *What can I do to turn things around and get back on the path to success and happiness?*

> *I was never given the opportunity to*
> *succeed, so I created my own.*
> —*Paul D. Forgay*

Remember, at every moment in your up-and-down life, *you are your greatest asset.* So what you do with yourself physically, mentally, financially, spiritually in your work and in your relationships, this is what sends that roller coaster *up high* and *down low.* Your personal and professional fortunes depend on the deployment of your

- *skills,*
- *habits,*
- *attitude,*

and how you tap into and utilize them. Given the opportunity, you must always try to capitalize on the upside of life. But whether you're up or down, it's essential to be of service to others. Never allow you—*your greatest asset*—to slowly sink away. Take action to save it at all costs, and your up-and-down life will be on the upswing.

> *Many know the bleak, miserable, dark rock*
> *bottom. Only a few find the strength to reach*
> *deep into their souls and rise up true champions.*
> —*Paul D. Forgay*

> *Hustlers have always maintained their*
> *modus operandi; a blend of hustling,*
> *steadfast determination, tenacious work*
> *ethic and overwhelming desire to succeed!*
> —*Paul D. Forgay*

CHAPTER 10

HAVE FAITH AND BE OF SERVICE

A grateful attitude can turn good into greatness.
—Paul D. Forgay

A symbol of hope, a touch of faith, and
a clear vision can bestow unrivaled
strength in unfamiliar circumstances.
—Paul D. Forgay

I was able to enrich my intellectual freedom by
challenging the boundaries of my domain.
—Paul D. Forgay

By now, I hope you understand that the way to achieve the most remarkable results in both work and life is to use all the tools you have *within yourself*—not wait for someone else or some outside force to improve your situation or circumstances. It's been my experience that I am the most capable person in any situation. I have confidence in that. I have *faith* in that, just as I have faith in God, and you should too (or in whomever your higher being is). Believing in yourself *always* provides consistency—and consistency is critical to building and maintaining a purposeful life.

For of all the adversity I've endured over the years, I finally decided that enough was enough, so I allowed my heart and passion to guide me through the many obstacles and struggles I've endured, and you will also endure through this journey called life. I wanted to contribute beyond me; *I chose to do whatever it takes to succeed, be of service to others, and cultivate a grateful heart.*

Achieving the understanding that *I am my greatest asset* has enabled me to realize that I am better than I think I am. That, in turn, has given me the confidence and courage to deal with and endure any kind adversity. There have been numerous times in my life that I've had to deal with adverse circumstances. In order to deal with these circumstances, I valued my heart over my mind. I speak from personal experience when I say that my belief that *I am my greatest asset* has not only changed my life; it has literally saved it— from failed relationships, mental illness, financial reverses, and other setbacks. And that's as real as it gets.

> *Rock bottom became the unshakable*
> *foundation on which I recreated my life.*
> —Paul D. Forgay

I relied on *my faith* to break through the hardships that I allowed to have an emotional impact on my life and turned me into the person I was not. So I decided to gently and quietly become the person I knew was living deep within inside of my heart. A person built on *FAITH, HUMILITY, HEART, PRAYER, COURAGE, GRATITUDE.*

One of the greatest challenges I have faced: mental illness. What do we do when we are faced with a diagnosis such as bipolar disorder, as I was? First, as startling as it sounds, such a diagnosis can also be liberating. The thing inside yourself that you have struggled with for years—the behaviors and urges that have held you back and discouraged you time and time again—has a name! You aren't the first person to suffer from this ailment, and you won't be the last. *You aren't alone.*

Sure, a mental disorder of this kind (or anything from a traumatic experience to an addiction) can threaten to incapacitate you. It can hamper your ability to work, think, live. It can even make you believe you'd be better off dead. "This is a disease that does not discriminate."

The reality is that this kind of illness is not like a cold or the flu. You can't just hang on and wait for it to go away. It will be with you in some form of life. The good news is, once you recognize it, you don't have to beat it! All you have to do is learn how to manage it—and certainly, even channel its energy in an encouraging and prosperous manner.

> *Successful sales professionals add substantial*
> *value when they provide absolute solutions.*
> —*Paul D. Forgay*

I struggle every day with my own disabilities. They have hurt me and left scars that can't be seen. I call these scars my "ghosts." They're there; you just can't see them. I am truly thankful for the scars my "ghosts it's because of them that I will be able to help others better understand that living with a mental health issue is not the end, but the beginning of an extraordinary journey only they can understand. But (with the help of professionals and especially *my greatest asset*) I have learned to harness the power of my unique psyche and use it as a tool to help me surpass my competition and exceed my goals. I will never, ever be outworked.

How can mental illness be a help rather than a hindrance in life? I promise you, it *can*. People like me, for example (people with bipolar disorder) tend to become abnormally focused on completing and repeating a task. I use that laser focus—I channel it—to help me solve problems at work and conquer even the most stubborn challenges in all aspects of my life.

Several years ago, I began carrying clothes, toiletries, and food in my car. I believed if I could hand out a little more each year, I would be able to reach my goal of feeding as many homeless, and those who are less fortunate, as possible. I began by handing out ten care packages the first year, Thanksgiving 2019. I was able to hand out fifty care packages: food, socks, shirt, sandwiches, protein bars, toothbrush, toothpaste, soap, shampoo, razor, shaving cream, and bottled water. I didn't want to just hand out food, I wanted to hand out items that would make others feel better about themselves, in the hopes of creating even the smallest of change. Let's face it, there's a massive homeless problem in this country. I believe there is a huge disparity between the haves and the have-nots. I want to make a difference, so I made it my goal that in ten years, I will be handing out five thousand care bags every year, and it is not only limited to holidays, but year-round. It's a lofty goal, but I feel an obligation to do something to help and be of service to others. It's not a lot, but it's a step in the right direction.

Paul—feeding the homeless

Just like me, you can turn a personal liability into an asset, adversity into opportunity. Start by taking inventory of your personal traits, those which you perceive to be weaknesses and strengths. Once you've identified them, think about how you can use them to your advantage benefit and how to best apply them in being of service to others. Challenge yourself to come up with positive applications for every trait you have—then go for it! Put your unique characteristics to work in your life and start living up to your full potential.

Only a life lived for others is a life worthwhile.
—Albert Einstein

A valuable lesson by a newspaper vendor:

Someone asked the richest man in the world, Bill Gates, "Is there anyone richer than you in the world?"

He replied, "Yes, there is a person who is richer than me."

He then narrated a story.

"It's during the time when I wasn't rich or famous. I was at New York Airport when I saw a newspaper vendor. I wanted to buy one newspaper but found that I don't have enough change. So I left the idea of buying and returned it to the vendor. I told him of not having the change. The vendor said, 'I am giving you this for free.' On his insistence, I took the newspaper. Coincidentally, after 2–3 months, I landed at the same airport and again I was short of change for a newspaper. The vendor offered me the newspaper again. I refused and said that I can't take it for I don't have a change today too. He said, 'You can take it, I am sharing this from my profit. I won't be at a loss.' I took the newspaper. After 19 years, I became famous and known by people. Suddenly, I remembered that vendor. I began searching for him and after about 1½ months of searching, I found him. I asked him, 'Do you know me?' He said, 'Yes, you are Bill Gates.' I asked him again, 'Do you remember once you gave me a newspaper for free?' The vendor said, 'Yes, I remember. I gave you twice.' I said, 'I want to repay the help you had offered me that time. Whatever you want in your life, tell me, I shall fulfill it.' The vendor said, 'Sir, don't you think that by doing so you won't be able to match my help?' I asked, 'Why?' He said, 'I had helped you when I was a poor newspaper vendor and you are trying to help me now when you have become the richest man in the world. How can you help match mine?' That day, I realized that the newspaper vendor is richer than me because he didn't wait to become rich to help someone."

People need to understand that the truly rich are those who possess a rich heart rather than lots of money.

It's really very important to have a rich heart to help others!

You must have faith—use the Shield of
faith to stop the fiery arrows of evil.
—Psalm 18:35

"If you are neutral in situations of injustice,
you have chosen the side of the oppressor."
—Desmond Tutu

Being of service to others is extremely important to me. The possessions that I am fortunate to have dictated that I have to go a lot further for those who are less-fortunate. I've given homeless people the shoes off my feet because—do I really need twenty-five pairs of shoes?

I save my empty plastic water bottles every day, and once I have several trash bags full of them, I take them to the local recycling center. But I don't recycle them and collect the deposit; I give them to the homeless.

One day, when I drove up to the recycling center with several large bags of used bottles, I came upon a husband and wife doing some recycling as well. They didn't seem homeless, but I could tell that they had very little. There was also a homeless man leaning up against a pole next to the recycling bin. He'd clearly passed out from drinking too much; the four empty 40s next to him gave it away.

I told the husband and wife that I would give them all of my empties with the understanding that they would leave the homeless man half the money, and they promised that they would. It was a superhot that day, so my next stop was a nearby grocery store, where I bought the three people I'd encountered some cold water and food—enough for several days.

When I returned to the recycling center, I found that the couple had already taken off. *That was fast,* I thought. Then I realized that they'd taken all of my plastic bottles and had not left anything for the still-dozing homeless man.

I shook my head in disgust. Then I did the math. I added up how much money they would get for the bottles, then compared it with the value of the food and water I had intended to give them. The amounts weren't even close. That husband and wife had made a very poor decision, not just morally but monetarily.

In the end, I left the homeless man half the food and water and gave the rest to an older couple living in their car. I thought about driving around looking for the people who had broken their promise to me but decided it was not worth the energy. I smiled as I drove away, understanding very clearly who in this story was fortunate and who wasn't as fortunate.

> *Don't underestimate the power of*
> *passion and raw emotion.*
> —*Paul D. Forgay*

CHAPTER 11

LISTEN AND CLOSE

Complacency is giving your competition
a clear path to victory.
—*Paul D. Forgay*

A successful salesperson will be quiet and listen.
—*Paul D. Forgay*

High performers consistently cultivate their
personal and professional growth.
—*Paul D. Forgay*

Listening rather than talking has become one of the most powerful sales tools of all time. I've learned and continue to learn how to apply these two words with the same six letters: L-I-S-T-E-N and S-I-L-E-N-T. Most people love to hear themselves talk. I've found listening to be as effective—or even more effective—than talking in many circumstances. *Listening* isn't just *hearing*; it is being able to process someone else's thoughts, perspective, and ideas and make them a reality. I've learned to listen calmly in order to fulfill the needs of others. Professional salespeople are skilled in the art of persuasion, highly knowledgeable, passionate, and charismatic and have the exceptional ability to turn a no into a maybe and a maybe into a yes. Attempting to close a business deal takes a great deal of patience and the unique aptitude to be able to listen to your internal conversations, at the same time listening to the potential clients' objections to your product and/or service.

It's been my experience that talking just to hear yourself talk is nonsense gibberish and can be very counterproductive. I have learned more and gained more from listening than I ever could from talking. When that guidance counselor sat across the desk from me and told me not to aim for college or a significant career, I listened carefully to what he said—and then did the exact opposite. (It's important to keep in mind that *listening* doesn't always mean *obeying*; it means actively processing what another person is saying, then following your best instincts.)

> *I've learned by experience that to take my*
> *career to the next level, it was imperative that I*
> *continually work on developing my listening skills.*
> —*Paul D. Forgay*

It's been my experience that a successful closer doesn't come by accident—having a tenacious work ethic; being an exceptional listener; thinking like a champion; be willing to take calculated risks; doing the things that others won't; always getting there before everyone else; staying hungry; being customer-focused, not competitor-focused; having a clear plan/vision; exceeding expectations; becoming a person of value; showing up every day and getting things done; being self-disciplined; having exceptional effort; being creative; and performing at an extremely high level of persistence and pure hustle. To weed out the weak and inexperienced closer, you must apply the aforementioned skills. You must set yourself up to win!

I put myself through an esteemed college and made a good life for myself and my family by listening to what that man said and *taking it for what it was worth*—and I am so glad I did. I have been listening carefully to those around me ever since. When it comes to listening, the devil is in the details. Listening closely and assessing what you hear carefully can mean the difference between success and failure—or even life and death.

Have I convinced you that there's merit in listening and learning from others? Be rigorous and tenacious in applying what you learn from listening because, without that step, the whole thing is of little value. It's been my experience that by listening intently while observing helps in better understanding your customers' needs. A good friend of mine once gave me some solid advice: "Sometimes the best business is the business you don't take." Over the years, I've walked away from a variety of business deals that seemed promising on the surface but that my due diligence and instincts told me weren't worth my time and effort. I listened to my friend's advice and still apply it today when faced with a potential venture or client. I usually make the right decision, and so can you, once you've cultivated the art of listening.

> *Exceptional sales professionals understand*
> *the importance of ingenuity.*
> *—Paul D. Forgay*

As the example of my guidance counselor demonstrates, just because you listen doesn't mean you have to take what you hear at face value. You have the choice to apply what you've heard, modify it, or reject it altogether and use it as inspiration for a different course of action altogether. Not everyone knows what he's talking about; not everyone is right. Before you accept someone's advice, recommendation, or even "facts," do your due diligence: ask other people and do your research. You might even want to do research on the person offering you the advice! I've learned a lot of the things and gained a lot of knowledge just by listening. I believe listening helps expand your imagination and creativity. And the greatest thing about listening is, it's free!

> *Pure salesmanship is an art form. You can*
> *either paint by numbers or be an innovator*
> *and paint like Leonardo da Vinci.*
> *—Paul D. Forgay*

Closing is an art form, a skill that is in high demand. A "professional closer" can command more money than an average salesperson, even a hard-working, intelligent, and determined one. If you want to get that order, that account, or whatever it is you are seeking, you have to *ask for it*. It's been my experience that the power of persuasion is a gift that only the most discipline person knows. A professional salespersons job is to continually invests in his or her own personal development, always acts with the best interests of the company and their customer above their own. At the end of the day a professional salesperson job is to is to turn a no into a maybe and a maybe into a yes.

Paul—giving presentation

An average salesperson struggles with closing a deal, but a great salesperson can make it happen, thanks to the skills they have acquired over time. By cultivating these skills, an average salesperson can become a phenomenal closer. Mediocre salespeople win awards, but great ones make bank. Great closers add extraordinary value to a company and turn customers into clients for life.

Be a person of value—added value adds
substance and substance increases revenue.
—Paul D. Forgay

I've been selling quality products and exceptional services for over four decades and have generated more than three hundred million dollars in sales. It has been my experience that to rack up exceptional numbers such as those, you must be passionate, believe in what you are selling, being true to your craft, create multiple streams of income, well versed in the art of persuasion and—perhaps most important—be a phenomenal closer. If your approach isn't working, change it up until you find one that does. If you're determined and persistent, you will find the right approach. It bears repeating: a phenomenal closer must be an excellent listener, patient but tenacious, passionate, and charismatic. And once you have honed your skills, you must practice them day in and day out. I have learned overtime that becoming a professional closer is not about making things easier, it's about making yourself better and being able to rise above the perception of your own limitations. I began to pray for hope and faith in order to learn how to be a resilient improved listener a successful entrepreneur must be an exceptional listener and closer.

A great salesperson listens in order to
familiarize himself with the needs of others.
—Paul D. Forgay

I firmly believe that the skills required for top-level salesmanship cannot be taught in a classroom; they must be acquired through experience, success, and failure. To put yourself in a position to learn and grow, you must hustle—another skill you cannot learn in a classroom.

The daily grind starts at two am; I am
not alone, hustle is by my side.
—Paul D. Forgay

A professional closer is someone who believes in their abilities, has a passion for what they do, and maintains a vision of what they want. That person achieves his goals. Closing a deal doesn't just apply to business; you can close a deal with yourself by conquering a fear, mastering a skill, or getting something, you go after. A closer in life can be a closer in business. Because of my relentless work ethic, I learned my way to success. I am not talented…just driven! Be a closer! I once had a goal of bench-pressing 300 pounds, but I only weigh around 165. Instead of making excuses, I stayed focused, passionate, persistent, believed in myself, and—this is important—*imagined myself doing it.* I worked out relentlessly, seven days a week; and while I did, I would close my eyes and envision myself bench-pressing 300 pounds. I remember the day I "closed the deal" on that goal. I was so focused that I exceeded it! I bench-pressed 325 pounds—almost twice my weight. *I closed the deal with myself.*

Paul—bench pressing

It's important to remember that, although you may be selling a world-class product and or service, you're ultimately your own brand. It is who you are and whom, what you represent and believe. The client will be looking for you to be a problem solver…

A good salesperson earns awards, but
a great salesperson earns bank.
—Paul D. Forgay

It's been my experience that cultivating connections is one of the most important aspects of doing business. That's as true today as it was in centuries past. Each person you know, in turn, knows a range of other people. Those friends of friends or colleagues of colleagues are connected to you—and that's a lot of connections! It pays to make and cultivate connections because they can turn into long-lasting professional and/or personal relationships.

Building and nurturing relationships can be as easy as joining a networking group or just asking the people you meet simple questions: What do you do? How long have you been doing it?

Do you belong to a networking group? Don't be shy, but don't be overbearing either. You can advertise as much as you want, but making connections may help you build your business even more effectively—and it won't cost you anything. This has certainly been true for me over the course of my career. I have made important connections through warehouse personnel, receptionists, drivers, salespeople—even janitors. And that is in addition to family friends, acquaintances, other parents at my kids' schools, people I run into at restaurants or social gatherings. You never know when you might meet someone who can help you—and they will do so unhesitatingly if you earn their respect. How do you do that? By respecting them. I can't emphasize enough how important it is to respect everyone, no matter what they do or how much money they make. Showing respect makes others feel they have value, are loved, and appreciated.

I've become so accustomed to treating others with the respect I desire in return that it has become a habit. What an awesome habit to have!

Overselling is a deal killer.
—Paul D. Forgay

CHAPTER 12

CREATIVITY AND RESOURCEFULNESS

Do not allow your deepest desires, dreams, or
ambitions to lay dormant in your soul. Be
diligent; let your creativity, resourcefulness
and imagination guide you. Then and only
then will you realize your true potential.
—Paul D. Forgay

Creativity is intelligence having fun.
—Albert Einstein

Be creative and discipline your thoughts, don't sell yourself short, and be willing to take calculated risks and never be satisfied with yesterday's triumphs. Keep grinding for a better tomorrow. I have read numerous books and articles throughout my life about bipolar disorder and ADHD. Research shows that having a mood disorder makes you more apt to creativity. It is also worth stating that people suffering from mood disorders will feel more tranquil in other areas, such as art, writing, and creativity; therefore their number will be subjectively high among the creative vocations. According to one investigation intelligence, creativity and bipolar disorder may share fundamental genetics. To be creative, you must think in a different way, and when we are different, we tend to be considered odd, crazy, and even insane. One possible explanation is that serious disorders of mood, such as bipolar disorder, are the price that human beings have had to pay for more adaptive behaviors such as intelligence, creativity, resourcefulness, and verbal expertise. As the world grows more complex, being different requires confidence. I learned at a young age that to become a successful entrepreneur and earn a remarkable amount of money, you must effectively leverage your experience, creativity, resourcefulness, and convey confidence.

> *To develop into a successful businessperson and earn an extraordinary income you must effectively apply your professional experience, innate creativity, and unmatched resourcefulness.*
> —*Paul D. Forgay*

Linking creativity to mental ailments—including bipolar disorder, ADHD, schizophrenia, depressive disorder, and anxiety disorder—is not an innovative idea. The connection between creativity and mental illness has been studied for centuries. It was Aristotle who associated the concept of insanity and genius together, maintaining that individuals with mental illness can see the planet in a creative, resourceful, and unique way particularly seeing things and imagining things others cannot. To be creative and resourceful, you must think with your unique mindset; and when we are unique, we tend to be labeled insane, crazy, and even eccentric. Your mindset is an authoritative tool—harness your hardships, drive your thoughts, and do not be afraid to be different.

I have learned that you can only go so far in life with a college degree; being naturally creative and resourceful is something that cannot be taught in a classroom.

One time, in high school, I was hanging out with my friends in one of their driveways. I remember it was a beautiful house. One of them said, "Paul, you're so poor that I could sell my car and buy your house." I knew he was right in one sense: my family didn't have any money or material things to speak of. But he was wrong too because we didn't even own our house—we rented.

I knew then and I still believe that having money doesn't make you better than the next person, but it can make it easier to take care of your family and give them a magnificent life. Money became my objective because money, in most cases is paramount in creating a sound monetary future. It can also mean fewer financial worries, enables you to give back to the community, just to name a few. Generally speaking, in order to acquire money, we must work; and in my case, that has meant working harder and smarter than others.

Through the eyes of a natural-born hustler.
—Paul D. Forgay

Today I am happy and grateful to be able to provide the basics of life for my family—food, water, shelter, and clothing—but I also strive to provide some of the finer items and to help others who are less-fortunate. I don't need a fancy car, a boat, or expensive jewelry, but there are some special things I feel are worth working for, such as travel, quality education, and enough security to feel free of fear.

Money not only allows us to buy nice things, helps in being of service to others; it can make our life less complicated when we're ready for retirement. As long as I can keep doing what I like, I'd be happy to work for the rest of my life while still being of service to others and taking some time off to travel and (someday) hang with my future grandkids. I've heard people say that money doesn't buy happiness, but it sure does make things easier.

Maybe you've been broke; maybe you're broke now. Well, I've been there myself, so I understand how the lack of money can make life extremely problematic. I am a natural-born hustler, a grinder, a twenty-four-seven-three-sixty-five *determined* individual, and I know one thing for sure: money don't lie!

Money is not the most significant thing in life, but money can make some of the most important things in life much better. That doesn't mean you can't have fun without money. When I was a kid, my friends and I would play football in the street until the sun went down. If there had been streetlights in our neighborhood that worked, we would have played even longer. Our end zones might be the front of an old yellow Ford Torino station wagon and an old-school Mustang—but we played hard, learned how to compete and had a blast.

Paul (right side)—Yellow Ford Torino

Entrepreneurs manifest their creativity
and their willingness to take calculated
risks to create significant value.
—Paul D. Forgay

Our game was supposed to be two-hand touch because we played on asphalt, but it always ended up being tackle, and we got banged up plenty. No matter, the bruises faded, but the memories of mixing it up with friends and family have lasted forever. No amount of money could ever buy those. These memories will forever be forged into my being.

Our biggest luxury in those days was a fake leather football from Zody's or Sears with the signature of either Roger Staubach or Terry Bradshaw stamped on the side. That and an occasional box of Band-Aids to stop the blood that tended to flow freely. Honestly, I wouldn't trade those memories for anything—certainly not money. That said, it's important to have clear financial objectives and work hard to achieve them. Cherish your friends and family, cherish your memories, but understand that money is one of the most important facets to a more fulfilling life.

> *Originality is creativity, brilliance,*
> *and the ability to unleash the most*
> *unimaginable power of one's mind.*
> —*Paul D. Forgay*

I've always known in my heart that I could defy any obstacle in my path because I was unique, believed in myself, and possessed exceptional skills, perseverance, heart, faith, and courage. I remain convinced that I have no limitations—that *I am my greatest asset.* I know from personal experience that people in a position of leadership—people with the power to influence those around them—should always strive to build others up. They should never tear them down, break their spirit, destroy their self-esteem, or diminish their hopes and dreams. Believe in yourself, avoid the noise and have a very clear vision for what you want out of life. I've learned that when you tap into and unleash your inner determination, creativity, and resourcefulness you too can TURN PAIN INTO TRIUMPH—ADVERSITY INTO OPPORTUNITY.

Adversity is not the enemy or a dream killer but a character builder, motivator, and personal-growth facilitator. The day I graduated from college, I looked up to the sky and thanked that guidance counselor who had told me I'd never amount to much—that I was lucky to be graduating from high school and I should grab any job I could get. Those words set me on a path of peak achievement. They provided me with one of the first *why* I had that my work ethic would define me.

For me, creative problem-solving is about analyzing a problem until you understand it, then finding the best way to resolve it. It is not always easy to break a problem down and figure out how to fix it—especially because people will attempt to sway you to their own views and opinions. Some of the most prosperous people in the world began their journey with little or no resources. People learn how to become more resourceful during their times of pain and adversity. If they could not find a way,

Resourcefulness is a common characteristic
amongst successful entrepreneurs.
—*Paul D. Forgay*

they created one. If you're resolute enough, you will find that resourcefulness is the greatest resource.

Let's say an employee has an issue with one of his or her colleagues. In order to sort it out, I have to get into a "problem-solving mind-set," analyze the situation, listen intently, and come to a clear understanding of it. Then I have to consider the best way to resolve it and apply that solution. Creative problem-solving is often done at a rapid pace, but careful consideration must always be a part of the process. I consider myself exceptionally good at being able to think swiftly on my feet. One reason that's true is that I work on myself regularly, through reading, exercise, prayer, meditation, listening to others speak, and honing my sales and interpersonal skills. The effort you expend on self-improvement is very worthwhile and will benefit your creative problem-solving process enormously. Working on myself enables me to have a larger vision of my dreams and goals, and it allows me to become a better version of myself. I have learned to become a person of value through constant self-development!

Sometimes creativity yields what you consider to be a *bad idea*—but no ideas are really bad because even something that proves unworkable in the end is part of the process that leads to the best possible solution. When I was attending college, I didn't have enough money for a computer, and it was challenging, carrying a full load in college, working forty to sixty hours a week, with my busy schedule, to use the computers in the school library. I had to find a way around this problem, or I wouldn't be able to finish my assignments and pass my classes. The creative solution I came up with was to invest what little money I had in a Brother electric typewriter. I went through a lot of Wite-Out, but you know what? The machine served my purposes, and

I completed all of my work on time. I could've simply made excuses, but I knew that was the path to failure, and that path was not for me.

High-level achievers recognize that resourcefulness is a necessary skill. It's about exhibiting ingenuity—creative problem-solving—in circumstances that demand it, sometimes right on the spot. It's about figuring out how to do more with less. Ask MacGyver! (Just kidding…but maybe not.)

Keeping an open mind and being proactive in unusual and chaotic circumstances are important to success in life. So is being able to think and act on a moment's notice. So is keeping an eye on the future and planning for it. All of these are aspects of *resourcefulness*. The way I see it, *resourcefulness is the ultimate resource*.

Creative problem-solving is a masterful skill
that is not easily learned but is in high demand.
This makes you that much more valuable.
—*Paul D. Forgay*

CHAPTER 13

JOURNEY BEYOND THE ORDINARY—
MY RICH LIFE EXPERIENCES

*The sky is not the limit; it is the
beginning of an epic journey.*
—*Paul D. Forgay*

*Once more into the fray...
Into the last good fight I'll ever know
Live and die on this day...
Live and die on this day...*
—*Jon Treloar*

My Journey Beyond the Ordinary began at a young age, not knowing I would be walking down a well-worn path, littered with an assortment of pain and adversity. I was unaware of all the great trials—great triumphs I would be faced with along this epic journey of mine. A story of passion, faith, adversity, darkness, hope, and the yearning to share it with others. I believe God planned for me to take this journey, a journey that was meant to be shared with family, friends, and strangers alike. This journey helped me discover what my real purpose in life is and that it's ok to be different!

I have often felt lonely in a crowded room, I've been laughed at, put down, used, stolen from, beaten, mentally abused, belittled, but I will never let anyone or anything keep me from living my dream.

It was incredibly important to me that I find my purpose and meaning in my own life. What can I learn during my epic journey? Will I become a better, more valuable person?

I have been blessed with my own unique inspirational life experiences, family, and friends, shattering my fears (what courage truly means), identifying my hero; humbled by my mistakes, time, knowing that money cannot buy heart or respect, having faith, and being of service to others is essential—the art of listening and closing, the value of being creative and resourceful, my epic journey beyond the ordinary (my rich life experiences)—each of these have given me the fortitude, grit, relentless work ethic, determination and self-discipline necessary to *turn pain into triumph and adversity into opportunity.*

> *It has been my experience that having the self-confidence to not just pursue success but strive towards becoming a person of value.*
> —*Paul D. Forgay*

Most of my life, I resented adversity of any sort (my own pity party), behaving miserably; and the woe was me syndrome. It felt like my mental state was being taken advantage of, punished the scapegoat for others lack self-awareness and for reasons I cannot fully understand or explain. I lived with mental illness every second, every minute, every hour, and every day for most of my life. I ultimately chose to share my rich life experiences with family and friends, so that I would no longer have to feel lonely in a crowded room.

I also had passionate moments of absolute attentiveness that would allow me to concentrate on my own rich life experiences. I finally accepted that there is no cure for my mental ailment, only treatment, but I kept fighting my way back, relentlessly pressing forward so that one day again, I would advance my own habits of success, phenomenal skills; can do attitude and my own self-affirmation that would improve and add exceptional value to my life and others.

I started to recognize that I was staring at my circumstances way too long I knew that I had to pick myself up, dust myself off, and begin by taking significant action. I had to discipline my thinking so I can lead by example, guide, inspire, and exemplify what it is to be a hardened warrior.

Let the past be the past; it's important that we learn from our mistakes, failures of our past and make use of them to inspire others; and that it is possible to write your own script.

It took me a long time to realize that I was being taken advantage regularly, by those who supposedly loved me the most. I became the fall-person for others and their inadequacies has created internal scars. I call them "ghosts"; they are there you just can't see them. Yet despite my mental ailments (adversity), I am still standing!

> *Hustling is not a nine to five job; it is a lifestyle*
> *that does not consist of punching a clock or*
> *working in a cubicle. Hustlers hustle 24/7/365!*
> *—Paul D. Forgay*

I work on raising the bar in my personal and professional life on a regular basis. My standard of excellence is essential to me because it is a direct reflection of the high expectations I set for myself. If I haven't set a high standard of excellence for myself or I am not working on raising that bar, I've accepted being ordinary and that is not acceptable to me. I've learned that sometimes when you find your purpose, or it may find you, it is just the beginning of a magnificent journey.

I have seen people get to the point where they feel they've reached their peak of excellence, so they stop growing. They have accepted the status quo. I choose not to accept the status quo because once I give myself permission to stop growing as a person, I will begin to die a slow and agonizing death—possibly without even knowing it's happening.

For me, continually raising my personal standard of excellence means listening to new ideas and taking from them what I believe works best for me while letting the rest just pass on by. Reading on a regular basis, taking care of myself physically, honing my creativity and imagination, continuing to believe in myself, and being of service to others are key to a more purposeful life. By raising my standards, I can accomplish what I set out to achieve, monitor what I might be able to improve on, and can both learn and teach others. All of this is imperative if I don't want to be left at the back of the pack. If you do not grow as a person, you will be left behind. If you're not raising the bar on your standard of excellence, you've given up. I will not be left behind because I expect to lead, and I will never give up or give into a life of perpetual mediocrity.

"How did you become such a good leader?"
someone asked Nelson Mandela.

"Because I learned to speak last,"
Mandela succinctly replied.

Be the last one to speak.
—*Nelson Mandela*

Most people who set both a personal and professional standard of excellence are committed to raising that bar continually. That means they are willing not only to learn but to share their wisdom with others.

My stream of consciousness allows me to enhance
my professional and personal growth continually.
—*Paul D. Forgay*

It's possible to become smart by studying hard and staying the course, but wisdom is not free and cannot be taught in a classroom, read in a book or social media; it must be experienced firsthand. Raising the bar and setting your standard of excellence can be very rewarding. I push myself. Sometimes I'm successful, and sometimes I fail; but if I don't drive myself or raise the bar, I know that I will become bored, unsatisfied, and not the person I strive to be. I know one thing for sure: my journey has never been boring, and it never will as long as I keep striving for higher levels of excellence.

There's a song by Rascal Flatts that I connected
with right away. The storyline of being "Changed."
Like me I got off track, I too made some mistakes.
The pain would not subside, I too hit my knees,
and now here I am, Here I am, changed!

I wasn't born to be a status quo; I was born to be a leader. It doesn't mean that I am better than other people. It means that I strive to be better than I ever thought possible. This inspires a sense of pride as I prove my naysayers wrong. Those naysayers don't bother me because I'm sure they have no knowledge or understanding of what it's like to experience such accomplishment. I choose to work on myself, create opportunities, set my standard of excellence, and raise the bar. It's a mind-set!

My Journey Beyond the Ordinary is not over—it is just the beginning—the new me—I am not finished with my purpose; I am just gaining momentum in sharing my stories of inspiration. I did not overcome my adverse situations alone, God was with me, by my side holding my right hand. You see God knows what I have been through and the challenges that lay ahead.

I don't have very much time these days so I'll make
it quick. Like my life. You know as we come to
the end of this phase of our lives, we find ourselves
trying to remember the good times and trying
to forget the bad times, and we find ourselves
thinking about the future. We start to worry,
thinking "What am I gonna do?", "Where am I
gonna be in ten years?" But I say to you, "Hey, look
at me." Please, don't worry so much, because in the
end none of us have very long on this earth—life is
fleeting. And if you're ever distressed, cast your eyes
to the summer sky when the stars are strung across

the velvety night, and when a shooting star streaks
through the blackness turning night into day, make
a wish and think of me. Make your life spectacular.
I know I did. I made it, mum! I'm a grown-up.
                                        —Robin Williams
                                        1951–2014

To access the most profound and obscure
aspect of your imagination, you must
allow your mind to flourish.
                                        —Paul D. Forgay

CHAPTER 14

TURN PAIN INTO TRIUMPH AND ADVERSITY INTO OPPORTUNITY

*I allowed pain, humiliation, "ghosts" my internal
scars, and adversity to occupy my soul, so that
I could establish triumph—opportunity and
purposeful life—being of service to others.*
                                    —Paul D. Forgay

"Only in the darkness can you see the stars."
                        —Martin Luther King Jr.

I have gone from sleeping in a 1964 VW square back to owning several thriving businesses, a five thousand-square-foot house on a hill with a breathtaking view, a sixty-five-foot houseboat, a ski boat, a Porsche 911 Carrera convertible, BMW's, dirt bikes, and a Harley. I've taken my family on first-class trips to Maui, Kauai, Mexico; Cabo San Lucas, Mazatlán, Puerto Vallarta. Whistler, British Columbia, Canada, Aspen, CO, Park City, Utah, The Alisal Guest Ranch & Resort, Santa Ynez Valley, CA, and Alaska. To name just a few. I've had a bulging 401(k) retirement fund, gold and diamond Rolex watches, gold and diamond jewelry, rare pearls, imported furniture, and a number of rental properties. And I've gone back to having absolutely nothing again—losing absolutely everything; twice, including my self-respect, my marriage, and almost my kids.

*The secret of happiness, you see, is
not found in seeking more, but in
developing the capacity to enjoy less.*
—*Socrates*

Ups and downs like these break most people and bring them to their knees. I almost let it happen to me. But I prayed, made the most of my *skills, habits,* and *attitude* and allowed my faith, gratitude and humility to guide me toward an understanding of *my greatest asset.* God had blessed me with three amazing kids, and they became my reason for picking myself up and fighting for my life. Not everyone has the courage or the ability to turn adversity into opportunity, but I dedicated myself to being one of the people who do. For me, this is not a cliché or something I read in a book. This is my life!

*Recognize the power of your personal,
compelling story and experiences.*
—*Paul D. Forgay*

Early in my life, I had decided that I could defy any obstacle in my path. I knew I could achieve greatness and be of service to others because I was unique, believed in myself, and possessed exceptional skills, talent, heart, faith, courage, passion, and a tenacious work ethic. I was convinced that I have no limitations because of my relentless work ethic and the mind-set that I would never be a victim of fear, failure, or the circumstances that created scars that would never heal (what I call my *ghosts.*) I knew then and I know now that my destiny is truly in my own hands and mind.

Paul—podcast

How you deal with adversity can be the
deciding factor between success and failure.
—Paul D. Forgay

Without goals a dream is just an illusion.
—Paul D. Forgay

My entire life, I've been able to inspire myself through my own rich life experiences—rich in the sense that money could never replace them, and they will be embedded in my heart, soul, and mind for eternity. Digging through trash cans, living in my car, experiencing psychological, physical, and substance abuse, losing everything not once but twice, and contemplating suicide—these are all a part of who I am. I am a better person for all of them.

There have been many times in my life that I've had an abundant amount of measurable success; at the same time feeling unhappy and unfulfilled. All through the pain I have experienced, I asked myself what can and will I learn from this pain. I learned what it is to be humbled, express much gratitude, have faith, and be of service to others. These are a few of the many reasons why I believe that my purpose in life is to share my rich life experiences and set an example for others. I want people to know my story and recognize that it's okay to be different, unique, and take risks. I want them to see by my example that they must have the courage and strength to talk about their adversities as they seek to overcome their hardships—that they can do it all by understanding and tapping into their *greatest asset*: themselves.

Whenever things get tough and you feel like quitting, encourage yourself with the following example of persistence.

He failed in business in '32.

He ran for the state legislature in '32 and lost.

He tried business again in '33 and failed.

His sweetheart died in '35.

He had a nervous breakdown in '36.

He ran for state elector in '40, after he regained his health.

He was defeated for congress in '43, defeated again for congress in '48, defeated when he ran for senate in '55, and defeated for vice president of the USA in '56.

He ran for senate again in '58 and lost.

Yet after all his failures, this man refused to quit. He kept trying until in 1860, he was elected president of the United states. This man was Abraham Lincoln.

The pain and adversity that I've endured have given me the strength to triumph and create my own opportunities. Pain and adversity not only changed my life, they literally saved it. And that's as real as it gets.

> *Do you feel the pain? It is a constant reminder*
> *that anything is possible through hard work*
> *and perseverance. Success is earned, not given.*
> —*Paul D. Forgay*

I still think about crawling under that chain-link fence with my friends Ruben and Oscar, lying on the front porch playing cowboys and Indians, playing football on the asphalt under the streetlights, and dancing to the Manhattans' "Oooh, yeah, honey, you are my shining star." I think about the Brother typewriter and Wite-Out. I think about the day I graduated from high school, the day I graduated from college, the day I started my first business, and the day each of my children was born. I think about the day I made my first million and the day I hit bottom, picked myself up, and started fighting my way back.

It's been my experience that if your *why* doesn't bring you to tears, it's just a mere thought and not your *why*. I wrote this book for many reasons, and I've told you most of them, but I also wrote it because I want my family and friends to know the real me, my story, that it's okay to be different—and, in fact, it can be the greatest blessing. I never want anyone I know—or any of my readers—to feel lonely in a crowded room!

CONTRIBUTE TO HUMANITY

UNWAVERING FAITH IN GOD

MY WORK ETHIC DEFINES ME

SKILLS, HABITS, ATTITUDE

TURN PAIN INTO TRIUMPH—ADVERSITY INTO OPPORTUNITY

YOU ARE YOUR GREATEST ASSET

FAITH, HUMILITY, HEART, PRAYER, COURAGE, GRATITUDE

IT'S YOUR LIFE, HOLD THE PEN AND WRITE YOUR OWN SCRIPT!

REVIEWS

Motivated and exudes an incredibly positive personality. Identifies problems, devises practical solutions, and the ability to inspire others. A highly intelligent person with a mind well-focused and the proven ability to help others achieve success.

—Marie
Business Executive

Paul delivers a powerful message that resonates with his audience.

—Phillip
Professor

Paul possesses an incredible work ethic, a great communicator, and a true professional. Exceptionally talented and has a great way with people. Presents creative solutions, infectious personality, and exceptionally inspiring.

—David
Business Owner and Entrepreneur

I have seen Paul tackle what seemed to be insurmountable tasks and personally. I understood the genuine care with which he approaches every aspect of his life. His dedication and perseverance have proven a valuable asset to my business. His extensive knowledge is an invaluable asset.

—Scott
Business Executive

Paul shares his personal life experience and how you too can turn adversity into prosperity. Exceptional message!

—Robin
Business Owner

Cowards die many times before their deaths; The valiant never taste of death but once.

—William Shakespeare

ABOUT THE AUTHOR

Paul D. Forgay, also known as PDF Inspires, is an author, motivational speaker, successful businessman, sales strategist and business consultant who decided early in life that he could defy any obstacle, Turn Pain Into Triumph—Adversity Into Opportunity, and inspire others through his own rich life experiences.

He has experienced failure and adversity on a multitude of levels throughout his life. He has lived in his car, dug through trash cans, faced physical and mental abuse, family violence, mental ailment, and others telling him that he would never amount to anything. He lost everything twice, contemplated suicide, made millions and lost millions. His story is a story of persistence, grit, faith, fearlessness, gratitude, and humility. He dedicated himself to do the things that others won't do; he refused to be cemented in the mediocrity of life. Paul believes his value is encased in his relentless work ethic. It's just who he is, and it's what he does. If the competition works forty hours a week, Paul works one hundred. If they start at 6:00 a.m., Paul starts at 4:00 a.m. They start at 4:00 a.m., Paul doesn't sleep. This is not something he thinks about doing. He lives it! He has endured and prevailed over his hardships with courage, tenacious work ethic, prayer, passion, faith, and humility to realize an otherwise incredible potential. But he is still here, and he believes his story is of great value to others. Paul's description of his life will strike a chord in many. He says there have been many times when he felt lonely in a crowded room. But through it all, he has held his head high and sought the strength that can only come from humility, gratitude, faith, and prayer.

Paul wants others to know his story so that they recognize that it is okay to be different, unique, take risks. It's your life, hold the pen and write your own script! He wants people to see firsthand that by summoning up the courage and strength to talk about their adversities, they will be able to overcome their hardships.

Paul believes his purpose in life is to represent the ideas of TURNING PAIN INTO TRIUMPH—ADVERSITY INTO OPPORTUNITY. He strongly believes if he can do it, so can you!

WWW.PDFINSPIRES.COM
PAUL@PDFINSPIRES.COM